Catholic Study Guides for Mary Fabyan Windeatt's

*Saint Dominic, Preacher of the Rosary
and Founder of the Dominican Order*

*The Children of Fatima
And Our Lady's Message to the World*

*Saint John Masias, Marvelous
Dominican Gatekeeper of Lima, Peru*

*Saint Benedict,
The Story of the Father of the Western Monks*

RACE for Heaven's Grade 6 Study Guides

Janet P. McKenzie

Biblio Resource Publications, Inc.
Bessemer, Michigan

Saint Dominic Study Guide © 2001 by Janet P. McKenzie
The Children of Fatima Study Guide © 2001, 2005 by Janet P. McKenzie
Saint John Masias Study Guide © 2004 by Janet P. McKenzie
Saint Benedict Study Guide © 2001 by Janet P. McKenzie

Catholic Study Guides for Mary Fabyan Windeatt's Saints Grade 6 © 2007 by Janet P. McKenzie

ISBN 978-1-934185-08-7
Second printing 2015

Published by
Biblio Resource Publications, Inc.
108 ½ South Moore Street
Bessemer, MI 49911
info@BiblioResource.com
www.BiblioResource.com

A **R**ead **A**loud **C**urriculum **E**nrichment Product
www.RACEforHeaven.com

Cover photo of Obelisk and Basilica in St. Peters Square, Rome © iofoto - Fotolia.com

Special thanks to Julia Fogassy from Our Father's House for her editorial assistance

Printed in the United States of America

Table of Contents

Spiritual Read Aloud

Spiritual Reading

In *My Daily Bread, A Summary of the Spiritual Life* by Father Anthony Paone, S.J., Christ tells us,

> My Child, reading and reflecting are a great help to your spiritual life. My doctrine is explained in many books. . . . Some of these books are written simply, and some are very profound and learned. Choose those which will help you most toward a greater understanding and appreciation of My Truth. Do not read to impress others but rather to be impressed yourself. Read so that you may learn My way of thinking and of doing things.

In her book, *Saint Dominic, Preacher of the Rosary and Founder of the Dominican Order*, Mary Fabyan Windeatt quotes St. Dominic as saying, "A little good reading, much prayer and meditation . . . and God will do the rest." Father Peter-Thomas Rohrbach, O.C.D., states that spiritual reading is the "third essential asset for mediation" (after detachment and recollection). The great value he places on the habit of spiritual reading is expressed in his book *Conversation with Christ, An Introduction to Mental Prayer*:

> We live in a world devoid, in great part, of a Christian spirit, in an atmosphere and culture estranged from God. Living in such a non-theological environment makes it difficult for us to remain in contact with the person of Christ and the true purpose of life itself. We must, if we are to remain realistically attached to Christ, combat this atmosphere and surround ourselves with a new one. Constant spiritual reading fills our minds with Christ and His doctrine—it creates this new climate for us.
>
> In former ages, spiritual reading was not as essential for one's prayer life. People lived in a Christian world and culture which was reflected in their laws, customs, amusements, and their very outlook on life. This situation has radically altered in the last two hundred years, and men must now compensate for this deficit through other media, principally reading. And as the de-Christianization of our world continues, the necessity for spiritual reading simultaneously increases. We stand in need of something to bridge the gap between our pagan surroundings and our conversation with Christ—spiritual reading fills this need.
>
> There is today in our country an alarming decline in general reading of all types. It has been estimated that in 1955 an astonishing forty-eight percent of the American adult population reads *no books at all*, and only eighteen percent read from one to four books. The decline in reading is naturally reflected in religious reading as well. And, while the lack of secular reading will occasion a decrease in culture life, the decline in religious reading

will have repercussions of a more serious nature—severe detriment to one's spiritual life. Any serious attempt to better one's life spiritually should, therefore, include the resolution to engage in more spiritual reading.

If we confine our reading to non-Catholic books, magazines and newspapers, we almost automatically exclude ourselves from full development in our prayer life. The maxims and philosophy of life expressed in these avenues of communication slowly begin to seep into our lives until eventually they occupy a ruling position. We will not have surrounded ourselves with a new climate; rather, the non-Catholic climate will have engulfed us.

As this decry of the "de-Christianization of our world" was written in 1956, one can safely surmise that the necessity of cultivating the habit of spiritual reading can only have grown in the past several decades.

Spiritual Read Aloud
As supported above, spiritual reading is an essential element of every Christian's life. However, as demonstrated by the ancient practice within monasteries of spiritual read-aloud, this habit is a powerful tool for shared community growth in the spiritual life. For Catholic families, the practice of reading spiritual books aloud produces four desirable effects:

I. It reinforces the habit of spiritual reading for each member of the family and allows each member to practice this habit regardless of age.
II. It reinforces the habit of spiritual conversation if the reading results in even a general discussion of the values and virtues being portrayed in the story.
III. It strengthens the family as the domestic Church where members exist to learn and live the Faith together for the support and enrichment of all family members.
IV. It allows the discussion and demonstration of the practical application of the Faith for all age levels.

The Habit of Spiritual Reading
As outlined above, establishing the habit of daily spiritual reading is essential to our spiritual growth. Through read-aloud, children can be taught at an early age that daily spiritual reading is a fun, rewarding exercise. Do make this time together pleasant by allowing the children to do crafts, draw, play quietly with puzzles, toys, etc. As long as their attention is not divided and they can participate in a discussion of the reading afterwards, allow quiet activity. One cannot expect children to sit piously with hands clasped prayerfully throughout the read-aloud session! As the children get older, encourage them to read other spiritual books, including the Bible, during a quiet time of their own. Model this habit by allowing them to observe your habit of daily spiritual reading as well. Although the family read-aloud sessions may be as long as thirty minutes, private spiritual reading times may be considerably shorter depending on the habits and temperament of each child.

The Habit of Spiritual Conversation
This habit, for many families, may begin with spiritual read-aloud. When each member of the family participates in a spiritual discussion of a religious book, the practice of discussing matters of faith and Christ-like living begins to form. If the formation of holy habits and imitation of the saints is the goal, these discussions will become common-place in the home as each member checks the others on their actions and words. As family members become more comfortable and open about spiritual matters, this practice will soon spread into other areas of their lives. Spiritual discussions with friends and other relatives will become more natural and in fact become important topics to be discussed. Sharing one's own spirituality and encouraging others to become more open about matters of faith will then become an integral pattern of living.

Strengthening the Domestic Church
As we read more about the saints and their lives and begin to share our faith more openly with others, we realize the importance of holy companionship—living with others who share our faith ideas and supporting each other in our attempts to become more like Christ. Families begin to grow together in their knowledge of the Catholic faith and become more willing to support each other throughout the ups and downs of community living. We begin to "bear one another's burdens with peace and harmony and unselfishness." Just as Christ has His Church to help bring salvation to all, we—as family members—have each other to provide mutual support and encouragement in our efforts to enter the narrow gate. Within our families, we can create the Catholic culture that is missing from our world's culture.

The Practical Application of the Faith for All Age Levels
When lives of the saints are read aloud in the family setting, all aged children can participate in a discussion of the imitation of the saint's virtues and holy habits. Each member can help others understand how to apply the lessons the saints teach us on a practical level. All family members can help choose a particular habit or virtue upon which to focus. A reward system can be established for virtuous behavior. A family "plan of attack" on non-virtuous habits and attitudes can be developed, implemented, checked, and revised. All members can be encouraged and taught to imitate Christ by the imitation of His saints.

Summary
Regular family read-loud sessions that center around the lives of the saints will benefit the family with an increased interest in reading—especially saintly literature, a growth in vocabulary, and an improved sense of family unity. Additionally, family members will be encouraged to develop the habit of spiritual reading on their own, will become more comfortable and experienced with spiritual conversation, and be able to apply the Truths of the Catholic faith, on a practical level, to all aspects of their lives—no matter what their age. The customs, habits, and attitudes of the family will more and more reflect those of the Catholic culture. Perseverance in this simple daily ritual will help to "bridge the gap between our pagan surroundings and our conversation with Christ."

When Mother Reads Aloud

When Mother reads aloud the past
Seems real as every day;
I hear the tramp of armies vast,
I see the spears and lances cast,
I join the thrilling fray;
Brave knights and ladies fair and proud
I meet when Mother reads aloud.

When Mother reads aloud, far lands
Seem very near and true;
I cross the desert's gleaming sands,
Or hunt the jungle's prowling bands,
Or sail the ocean blue;

Far heights, whose peaks the cold mists
    shroud,
I scale, when Mother reads aloud.

When Mother reads aloud I long
For noble deeds to do—
To help the right, redress the wrong,
It seems so easy to be strong, so simple
    to be true,
O, thick and fast the visions crowd
When Mother reads aloud.
    –Anonymous

The Reading Mother

I had a mother who read to me
Sagas of pirates who scoured the sea,
Cutlasses clenched in their yellow teeth,
"Blackbirds" stowed in the hold beneath.

I had a mother who read me plays
Of ancient and gallant and golden days
Stories of Marmion and Ivanhoe,
Which every boy has a right to know.

I had a mother who read me tales
Of Gelert, the hound of the hills of
    Wales,

True to his trust till his tragic death,
Faithfulness blest with his final breath.

I had a mother who read me things
That wholesome life to the boy-heart
    brings—
Stories that stir with an upward touch,
O, that each mother of boys were such.

You may have tangible wealth untold,
Caskets of jewels and coffers of gold.
Richer than I you can never be—
I had a mother who read to me.
    –Strickland Gullilan

How to Use These Study Guides

✤REVIEW✤ Vocabulary

Vocabulary words are listed at the beginning of each lesson. Words on the left are secular words and are given within the sentence structure. Allow students to guess the meaning of the italicized word before looking it up. This helps them to surmise the meaning from context, a skill that enhances reading comprehension and strengthens vocabulary. Vocabulary words listed in the right-hand column are Catholic vocabulary words. Help students identify any suffixes, prefixes or root words that might give clues to the word's meaning. To help with definitions and proper usage, use a dictionary. For Catholic vocabulary words, use a Catholic encyclopedia, dictionary, or catechism.

??? Comprehension Questions/Narration Prompts

These questions are appropriate for all age levels. They can be used several ways, depending on a student's ability. For students with difficulty in reading comprehension, read and briefly discuss these questions before reading the chapter. Discuss, too, the sub-title provided under each chapter heading in the study guide. The student will then know what content to watch for within the reading. If read afterward, the questions become a *test of,* rather than an *aid to,* comprehension. For students with adequate comprehension skills, use the questions for oral review after the reading to insure that important content has been absorbed.

Use these questions too as prompts for narration, which is simply the oral retelling of the story in the student's own words. It is a helpful tool to determine the level of each student's comprehension. All ages may benefit from the practice of narration. If done within a mixed age group, begin with the youngest students and have the older students add details to the already-related story.

Answers to comprehension questions are provided in the answer key.

💡 Forming Opinions/Drawing Conclusions

More than relating events, these questions require the student to develop an opinion, or to uncover or discover material not expressly stated in the text. They are designed to develop thinking skills and do not usually require the use of any outside resources. Use this section with children grades five and up as the basis for discussion or as a writing assignment.

📖 For Further Study

Appropriate for upper elementary through high school grades, this section requires the use of additional reference materials. These activities invite students to look more deeply at the historical events and people that shaped the times of each character. Topics in this section may be used for honing research skills, or for oral presentations and/or written reports.

✝ **Growing in Holiness**

These activities are different from the others in that they do not involve discussion or study as much as personal action and interior reflection. They can perhaps be considered "conversion activities" or "life lessons." By applying the spiritual lessons of the story to everyday life, the student is encouraged to develop habits in imitation of the saints—which is an imitation of Christ Himself. Remember to reinforce these activities with the student and to comment when they are observed in action.

Geography

The map provided with this study guide serves to orient the students with respect to space—*where* the action of the story is taking place—as well as to acquaint them with common geographical landmarks. Permission is hereby granted to photocopy maps for family or classroom use.

Timeline Work

The creation of a timeline allows students to place the story's events within a wider historical framework. Simple directions for making a timeline are included in the study guide. Students will need plain paper, colored markers, and a ruler.

✓ **Checking the Catechism**

For older students, these activities require a copy of the *Catechism of the Catholic Church* (*CCC*) or its *Compendium*. The references for the more concise *Compendium* appear in parentheses after the *CCC* citations. Older students can read aloud—and then discuss—the stated text paragraphs with an adult.

For younger students, use any grade-appropriate catechism to review the doctrines and terms as specified. An excellent activity book for multi-grades is Ignatius Press' *100 Activities Based on the Catechism of the Catholic Church* by Ellen Rossini. Discuss together how the specific topics from the catechism are illustrated in the thoughts and actions of the characters in the book.

Searching Scripture

Familiarize the student with the inspired Word of God by studying the biblical passages provided. Strengthen these exercises by occasionally requiring memorization of the verse(s). Stress that knowledge of Scripture is an important part of our faith education.

Note that Ms. Windeatt used the Douay-Rheims translation of the Bible, which was the translation in use in the United States until 1970 when it was replaced by the New American Bible in the *Lectionary of Mass*. The Douay-Rheims translation is taken from the Latin Vulgate, whereas the New American translation comes from the original languages of Hebrew, Aramaic or Greek (as the case may be for each specific book). For this reason, some of the books' names (as well as some of the Psalms' numbers) differ between these two translations. When these differences occur in the biblical citiations within this study guide, the New American references are given first with the Douay-Rheims references following in parentheses. All biblical references used in this study guide are from the New American translation.

✎ Test

The purpose of the test is to ensure that the student has comprehended the important events in each saint's life as well as the lessons the story intends to impart. An answer key is provided for these questions.

In addition to the test, many students will benefit from the completion of a book report. See RACE for Heaven's *Alternative Book Reports for Catholic Students* for additional information on book reports specifically geared toward saint biographies. Consider requiring each student to choose one of these reports or activities upon completion of the Windeatt biography.

Warning

These study guides are comprehensive. They contain activities for a variety of age levels and areas of study. Do **not** attempt to complete every activity for every lesson. Do only those exercises that are suitable for the needs of your current situation. Resist the impulse to be so thorough that the story line of the book is lost, and the read-aloud sessions become dreaded rather than anticipated. The activities are designed to enhance your reading—not to become the dictating tyrant of your read-aloud time together. If you are using these guides for young audiences, consider just using the comprehension and opinion questions as well as the "Growing in Holiness" section; use the maps as a geographical visual aid. Re-read the books to complete the more advanced activities in later years.

Another suggestion is to use the activities designed for older students in coordination with their history, geography, writing and/or religious curriculum. Each study guide could also be used as a complete unit study for hectic times when regular school may not be in session such as Advent, times of family stress (the birth of a new sibling, for example) or over the summer months. In reading the book and completing the activities, subjects such as religion, reading, writing, geography, and history can all be easily covered.

The most important rules to the successful use of these enrichment activities are

1. Be creative rather than obsessive.
2. Be flexible rather than overly structured.
3. Enjoy!

Study Guide for

Saint Dominic,
Preacher of the Rosary
and Founder of the
Dominican Order

St. Dominic

St. Dominic de Guzman was born in Spain.
He wanted to preach in Tartar terrain.
But no far-off lands,
Instead heretics' bands,
In nearby France was where he must remain.

To speed their conversion, he tried to recruit
Women in convents who prayed he'd bear fruit.
Where others had failed,
Dominic prevailed.
The Spirit was with him and soon Truth took root.

He battled the devil and beat him no sweat.
He started an order. St. Francis he met.
Then after a vision,
He made a decision.
He preached while in Rome, tide of sin to abet.

His order soon flourished; his fam'ly did grow.
The angels would feed them when supplies got low.
He spoke to the wise—
The real learned guys.
By Dominic's preaching, these men Truth did know.

His priests were great leaders; they stood by his side.
To praise, bless, and preach by this motto abide.
And *Veritas*—truth—
For old and for youth—
On this motto too the Dominicans relied.

The Mother of Jesus was Dominic's friend.
She gave him her ros'ry to pray without end.
So faithful was he
That when he would plea
The powers of this world his prayers would transcend.

Think what you can learn from this saint and his tale.
How you can apply it to help you prevail.
Then mold what you do
And boldly pursue
His pattern of holiness. Follow his trail.

Timeline of Events

Year	Event
c. 1120	Playing cards invented in China around this time
1154	House of Plantagenet rules England
1155	Carmelite Order founded
1168	Beginning of Aztec migration
1170	Birth of Dominic de Guzman; murder of St. Thomas á Becket
1174	"Leaning Tower" built at Pisa, Italy
1179	Third Lateran Council
1185	Japan begins 700 years of military rule (Shogun/Samurai)
1189-1197	Third Crusade led by Richard the Lion-Hearted
1193	Birth of St. Albert the Great (died 1280)
1194-1260	Erection of Chartres Cathedral
1195	Ordination of Dominic
1198	Peak of the medieval papacy
1202-1204	Fourth Crusade
1206	Dominic establishes a religious community of women at Prouille, France
1206-1227	Genghis Khan chief prince of Mongols
1208	Our Lady presents Dominic with the rosary
1208-1229	War against the Albigenses
1209	St. Francis establishes the first rules for the Franciscans
1212	Children's Crusade
1214	Dominic establishes his order—the Order of Preachers
1214	Birth of Roger Bacon, Franciscan monk and English philosopher (died 1294); Genghis Khan crosses Great Wall of China
1215	Fourth Lateran Council—the "Great Council"; Magna Carta signed by King John
1216	King John of England dies; reign of Henry III begins
1218	Dominic appointed as first Master of the Sacred Palace (pope's theologian) by Pope Honorius III, a position held since by Dominicans; Pope Honorius III asks Dominic to unite the communities of nuns in Rome; Reginald joins the Dominican order; our Lady presents the order's habit
1220	Hyacinth and his companions meet Dominic and join the Dominican order
1221	Death of St. Dominic; City of Vienna founded
1225	Birth of Thomas Aquinas
1228	St. Francis, who had died in 1226, canonized by Pope Gregory IX
1230	Wenceslas, King of Bohemia (until 1253)
1231	Papal Inquistition; death of Anthony of Padua
1234	St. Dominic canonized by Pope Gregory IX
1247	First Council of Lyons
1251	Simon Stock sees vision of our Lady and is given the Brown Scapular
1256	Beginning of the Hundred Years' War between Venice and Genoa
1268-1271	Three-year vacancy in the papacy
1270	Marco Polo journeys to China

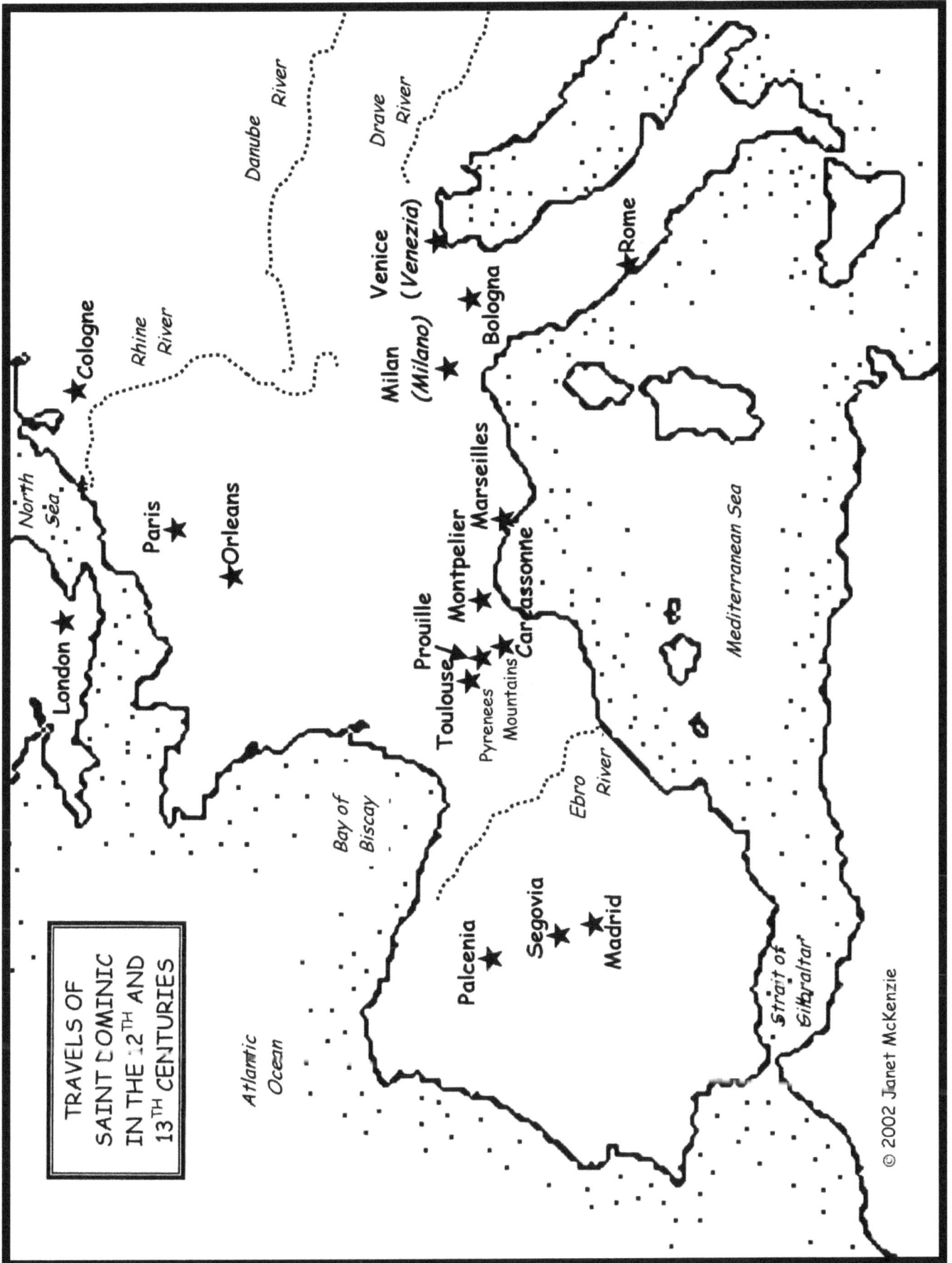

TRAVELS OF
SAINT DOMINIC
IN THE 12TH AND
13TH CENTURIES

Danube River

Drave River

Rhine River

Venice (Venezia)

Rome

Cologne

Milan (Milano)

Bologna

North Sea

Paris

Orleans

Marseilles

London

Montpelier

Carcassonne

Prouille

Mediterranean Sea

Toulouse

Pyrenees Mountains

Bay of Biscay

Ebro River

Segovia

Madrid

Palcenia

Atlantic Ocean

Strait of Gibraltar

Chapters 1 and 2–In Which Dominic Travels with Bishop Diego and Begins His Work of Preaching to the Heretics

✖✖✖✖ Vocabulary
sent out an almost constant *dirge*　　*heretics*
salvation of thousands is in *peril*　　*sacrilege*

⁇⁇ Comprehension Questions/Narration Prompts
1. For what did Dominic sacrifice his books?
2. What was Bishop Diego's attitude regarding his desire to become a missionary to the Tartars in eastern Europe?
3. Why did Dominic and Bishop Diego travel to Rome to see Pope Innocent the Third? (Remember that this is a long journey, which took over a month to walk.)
4. In what state did Dominic and Bishop Diego find the missionaries in Montpellier?

💡 Forming Opinions/Drawing Conclusions
1. Bishop Diego tells Pope Innocent the Third of his desire to suffer martyrdom (page 11). Explain why he—or any Christian—would wish to be killed for his faith.
2. List the two suggestions Bishop Diego gave the abbot of Citeaux to increase the number of conversions experienced by the monks. Analyze how and/or why these suggestions might be helpful.

✝ Growing in Holiness
"A small act performed through holy obedience is of far more value in the eyes of God than a great act performed without it" (page 11). This means that God is more pleased with our obedience to the simple requests of our parents than any sacrifice or act of charity that we make on our own. Be mindful of your strict and cheerful obedience to your parents and others in authority over you this week.

🗓 Timeline Work
Taping sheets of plain paper end-to-end, make a timeline representing the years from 1120 through 1270. Let three inches equal 25 years. Mark on your timeline the dates and events from 1120 through 1204, using information from page 2 of this study guide.

📖 Searching Scripture
Bishop Diego quotes Jesus, "Lord, not my will but Thine be done!" (page 3). Read this quotation in context in Luke 22:42.

Chapters 3 and 4–In Which Dominic Hears the Blessed Mother Speak in His Heart and Founds a Religious Community for Women

---

✖REVIEW✖ Vocabulary

the stone *citadel* of Carcassonne   *Superior*
doctrines . . . were being *fostered*   *surplices*

??? Comprehension Questions/Narration Prompts

1. What were the heretics teaching children in their schools? What did Dominic and the other monks hope to do to counteract this?
2. What characteristic of Dominic's made him a logical choice for superior?
3. The 150 Hail Marys of the complete fifteen-mystery rosary borrowed its number from what?
4. Name at least three places where Dominic's missionaries preached.
5. To whom did Dominic turn when confronted by the group of women heretics?
6. What finally convinced these women that Dominic was speaking the Truth?

✠ Growing in Holiness

Dominic speaks of how short the complete rosary ("Our Lady's Psalter") is compared to reciting the 150 Psalms. He speaks of the power of this prayer, indicating that it can be recited while walking to and from work, or by peasants and little children. If you have not yet established the worthy habit of a daily family rosary, begin now. If this is not possible, begin to recite at least five decades of the rosary by yourself each day. Remember to meditate on the mysteries of our redemption while reciting the prayers.

✓ Checking the Catechism

Dominic speaks of the "one true Church" (page 24). Younger students may review the marks of the Church in their catechisms. Older students may read text paragraphs 811-13, 823-26, 830-31, 846-848, 857-62, and 866-70 (161-176) in the *Catechism of the Catholic Church (CCC)*. If desired, complete Activity #47 of *100 Activities Based On the Catechism of the Catholic Church*.

📖 Searching Scripture

1. Read about the "first and worst of lies" (page 25) in Genesis 3:1-15.
2. Bishop Diego explains that "active work such as preaching is of little use without prayer and good works behind it" (page 29). Cloistered nuns and monks provide this support for active missionaries. Read Colossians 4:12-13.
3. Research the life of St. Mary Magdalen by reading Matthew 27:56 and 28:1-8, Mark 15:47 and 16:1-11, and John 20:1-2 and 20:11-18.

Chapters 5 and 6–In Which Dominic Continues to Convert the Albigensians during the War and Challenges Them to Kill Him

✘REVIEW✘ Vocabulary
never *deigned* to listen   *friar*
hordes of ruthless *brigands*   *indulgences*

??? Comprehension Questions/Narration Prompts
1. What Albigensian heretic challenged Pope Innocent III?
2. Why did Dominic go to Carcassonne? Why did he go to Rome? Who did he meet there?
3. What happened in Prouille in mid-April of 1216?

Forming Opinions/Drawing Conclusions
Compare and contrast the religious orders of Dominic and Brother Francis.

For Further Study
Research the Fourth Lateran Council, which was convened by Pope Innocent III in 1215; this council was also called the "Great Council."

✝ Growing in Holiness
Try to gain at least one plenary indulgence per week. Remember that you must receive Holy Communion on the same day as you complete the act or prayers to which the indulgence is attached as well as recite one Our Father and one Hail Mary for the intentions of the Holy Pontiff. Below are some examples of prayers or practices to which a plenary indulgence is attached.
1. Pray five decades of the rosary in church or pray a family rosary
2. Pray the Stations of the Cross in church
3. Adoration of the Blessed Sacrament for at least one-half an hour
4. Read Scripture for one-half hour
(For additional suggestions, see the *Handbook of Indulgences, Norms and Grants*.)

Geography
Trace the map on page 3 of this study guide. Color the seas blue: Atlantic, North, and Mediterranean as well as these rivers: Rhine, Danube, Ebro, and Drave. The remainder of the map will be completed in Chapters 11 and 12.

Searching Scripture
"Cast your cares upon the Lord and He will sustain you" (page 45). Read Psalm 55 (54):23 and 1 Peter 5:7.

Chapters 7 and 8–In Which Dominic Founds His Order of Monks and Sends Them Out to Establish Convents

---

⭐REVIEW⭐ Vocabulary

still *unlettered* men and boys   *pontiff*
must be a *simpleton*   *consecrate*

??? Comprehension Questions/Narration Prompts

1. What was Dominic's second vision while at the Basilica of St. Peter?
2. What honor did Pope Honorius III bestow upon Dominic after giving his blessing for Dominic's new order of monks?
3. What two cities were the first sites for Dominic's new convents?
4. For what did Brother Stephen ask when overwhelmed with new responsibilities?
5. According to Dominic, what is the most valuable gift anyone ever gave us?

Forming Opinions/Drawing Conclusions

1. Explain the positive and negative aspects of Dominic's dispersal of his monks so far and so fast.
2. In your opinion, was Dominic right to give Brother John the bag of coins before his trip? Support your argument.

✝ Growing in Holiness

Dominic stressed a knowledge and love of God over book learning. Make sure your studies include time for prayer—"a little good reading, much prayer and meditation" (page 58). The reading to which he refers is brief passages from the Gospels; "remember the Divine Presence within yourself . . . then call frequently upon the Holy Spirit for help in understanding and putting into practice what they contain" (page 59). Make time for spiritual reading and reflection each day.

✓ Checking the Catechism

Brother Lawrence speaks of the Holy Spirit as the "Spirit of Wisdom" (page 59). Younger students can study the Holy Spirit and His gifts in their catechisms. If desired, complete Activity #8 in *100 Activities*. Older students can read text paragraphs 1830-33 (389-390) in the *CCC* on the gifts/fruits of the Holy Spirit.

📖 Searching Scripture

1. Brother Stephen requests Dominic to pray for him. Read these passages which speak of our prayers for each other: Philippians 1:3-7, and 1 Thessalonians 1:2-3.
2. Read too Romans 8:26-27.
3. Dominic explains the great gift of salvation and the role the Blessed Mother plays in God's plan. Read the story of the Annunciation in Luke 1:26-38.

Chapters 9 and 10–In Which Reginald Joins the Friars, and Dominic Performs Miracles

___

✖✖✖✖✖ Vocabulary

doffed the linen surplices   *Confraternity*
the *larder* was bare   *Holy Sepulcher*

??? Comprehension Questions/Narration Prompts

1. Pope Honorius III gave the monastery of St. Sixtus to Dominic in 1218. What favor did he ask in return?
2. Why was Reginald making a pilgrimage to the Holy Land?
3. What was the "secret" to Dominic's success as a preacher?
4. What was the title that Mary gave to Dominic's monks when she replaced the linen surplice with the white woolen scapular?
5. How did the community miraculously get fed when food was short?

Forming Opinions/Drawing Conclusions

1. List the things that Reginald would have to give up to enter the monastery. Discuss the sacrifices of entering a religious order or becoming a priest. What are the rewards?
2. Why do you think Dominic was pleased that the novices had given away the last loaf of bread? Which is easier—to trust in God or to rely on our own resources to provide?

For Further Study

Research the distinctive habits of the Dominicans. Why are their habits black and white? From where did the term "Blackfriars" come?

✝ Growing in Holiness

Dominic was able to raise Gutadona's son from the dead by making the Sign of the Cross over him. This simple prayer professes our belief in the Holy Trinity as well as Christ's redemptive act of dying upon the cross for us. Become aware of the powerful words of this prayer; it is more than a mere beginning and end to other prayers. Begin to pray devoutly the Sign of the Cross as a prayer within itself. Set up a holy water font in your home to add more grace to this action.

Timeline Work

Add the dates and events from 1206 through 1218 to your timeline.

Searching Scripture

Crowds often pressed upon Dominic when he preached. Read how the crowds pressed upon Jesus: Matthew 13:1-2; Mark 2:1-4 and 10:13-16; and John 6:2.

Chapters 11 and 12–In Which Brother Reginald Gathers More Souls at Bologna, and We Learn the Story of Blessed Diana

✲REVIEW✲ Vocabulary
in direct *contradiction*
Standing in the *pulpit*

holy poverty
Augustinians

??? Comprehension Questions/Narration Prompts
1. What tradition did Dominic's friars change to commemorate the angels' visit to the monastery with the loaves of bread?
2. On what topic did Brother Reginald speak in an attempt to increase the number of people coming to hear him preach in the church of St. Mary of Mascarella?
3. To whom was Brother Reginald compared? Why?
4. What did Diana arrange to show her appreciation for Brother Reginald's counsel?
5. Explain the vision Dominic receives of Diana as she gave herself to God?

✝ Growing in Holiness
Recite the guardian angel prayer each day. Name your angel and ask your angel's help often, especially in times of temptation and troubles. Remember to send your angel on journeys for you to watch over those you love or to sit before the Blessed Sacrament for you when you are unable to go yourself. Keep your angel very busy working for you and the salvation of other souls!

Geography
Complete the map started in Chapters 5 and 6 by labeling the cities red. On the map provided, cities are indicated with a star. Using a modern map, label the countries' names in which these cities are now located. Color the mountains yellow.

✓ Checking the Catechism
Younger students may study references in their catechisms to the angels (good and bad). Using the back index, older students should reference "angels" in the *CCC*. If desired, have students complete Activity #42 in *100 Activities*.

📖 Searching Scripture
1. Compare and contrast the feeding of the friars with the multiplication of the loaves and fishes in the Bible as well as Jesus' first miracle at Cana. Use these passages for reference: Mark 6:34-44 and 8:1-9; and John 2:9-10.
2. Read the following Bible passages regarding angels: Psalms 8:5-6; Psalms 91 (90):11-12; Psalms 103 (102):20-21; Matthew 18:10; and Colossians 1:16.
3. "I am here because I am learning to love" (page 98). Review 1 Corinthians 13:13. Find other Bible passages that relate to the importance of love.

Chapters 13 and 14—In Which Dominic Organizes the Nuns' Communities of Rome and Raises Napoleon Orsini from the Dead

---

✱REVIEW✱ Vocabulary

Seasoned traveler that he was
downright *imprudent*

feast
Lateran

??? Comprehension Questions/Narration Prompts

1. Holiness depends, in a large measure, upon what?
2. What task had Honorius III given to Dominic?
3. State why Mother Eugenia did not want to move her community of nuns.
4. What convinced the sisters of St. Mary's to move to St. Sixtus and adopt the rule prepared by Dominic?
5. To what does Dominic attribute true happiness in this life?
6. Describe the miracles related in Chapter 14.

Forming Opinions/Drawing Conclusions

Discuss the value of suffering in the Christian life. What role does it play? What demands does it make? What rewards does it offer?

For Further Study

Dominic carried St. Luke's picture of our Lady to the sisters' new home. Read about the legend and view this picture online at www.marypages.com. (Select "Perpetual Succor, Our Lady of" on left column.)

Growing in Holiness

It was at the moment of the Elevation at Mass that Dominic was himself miraculously elevated. Whenever you assist at Mass, be mindful of the miracle that occurs at every Mass: bread and wine become Jesus Himself—His Body, His Blood. He loves you so much that He wishes to be physically present in you. He loves you so much that He is the Divine Prisoner Who remains ever-present in the tabernacle.

✓ Checking the Catechism

Dominic speaks of the goodness and kindness of God (page 115). In their own catechism, younger students should study the perfections of God. Older students may study this topic in the *CCC* in text paragraphs 210, 238-39, 300, and 370 (39, 50, 416, and 592).

Searching Scripture

"Young man, in the Name of Our Lord Jesus Christ—arise!" (page 123) Read about Jesus raising the widow's son in Luke 7:11-15 where similar words cause a miracle.

Chapters 15 and 16–In Which Hyacinth and His Companions Join Dominic's Order, and We Learn of Dominic's Youth

⟪REVIEW⟫ Vocabulary

their fears and *scruples*   *inclosure* (or *enclosure*)
happy *musings* about the future   *Matins*

??? Comprehension Questions/Narration Prompts

1. Who did Dominic feel would succeed him as head of the Order of Preachers?
2. What did Bishop Ivo Odrowatz ask of Dominic? What was Dominic's response?
3. What was the mission of Dominic's order?
4. What did Dominic tell Bishop Ivo is the best gift we can give each other?
5. Name Dominic's two brothers.

💡 Forming Opinions/Drawing Conclusions

Briefly relate the story of the vision Dominic's mother had about him. What is the symbolism of this story?

For Further Study

"Sister Cecilia and Sister Amata, like Diana, would be revered as 'Blessed' by the entire Order of Preachers" (page 137). Research the three-step process for the canonization of saints in a Catholic dictionary/encyclopedia or online. Research the following terms: "venerable" (the person is now called "Servant of God"), "beatification" (the person is referred to as "Blessed"), and "canonization" (the person is now known as "Saint"). What are the requirements for each step?

✝ Growing in Holiness

"'My children, ask for these graces!' he implored. 'Ask! Ask! Ask! The Blessed Mother never fails to hear us when we beg her help . . .'" (page 138). Pray the Hail Mary very slowly, pausing after each phrase to mediate on the meaning of the words. What makes this prayer so powerful?

Timeline Work

Add the events from 1220 through 1270 to complete your timeline.

📖 Searching Scripture

Dominic acts in imitation of Jesus when He calls forth unlikely candidates for his work. Read about Jesus' gathering of the twelve apostles in Matthew 4:18-22 and 9:9; and John 1:35-49.

Chapters 17 and 18–In Which Dominic Establishes the Secular Third Order of Dominicans and Dies a Holy Death

---

⟨REVIEW⟩ Vocabulary

undertake a *campaign*   *Missal*
the apostolic *legate*   *Master of the Sacred Palace*

⁇⁇ Comprehension Questions/Narration Prompts

1. What is the "Militia of Jesus Christ"?
2. What two mottoes did Dominic adopt?
3. Where did Dominic wish to die and be buried?

💡 Forming Opinions/Drawing Conclusions

1. "Apostles, every one of them!" (page 145). Describe apostles and explain what they do.
2. Discuss why the two mottoes for Dominic's order are appropriate choices. Cite incidents from his life and the life of his friars to support your argument.
3. List events and actions from Dominic's life and death that reinforce his teachings of holy poverty and holy obedience.
4. Much of St. Dominic's life was spent fighting the heresy of the Albigenses. Why it is important to know the truth of the Catholic faith in order to defend against heresies? Why is it important that each of us know the doctrines of the Church as well as the false doctrines of the heresies against the Church?

✠ Growing in Holiness

The last testament of St. Dominic was his exhortation to "have charity among you; hold to humility; keep willing poverty" (page 154). Determine at least three things you can do to keep charity within your household, three things you can do to hold to humility, and three things to keep willing poverty. Do them.

✓ Checking the Catechism

Older students should read text paragraph 956 in the *CCC* which quotes Dominic's dying words as related to the doctrine of the communion of saints. Younger students may study the communion of saints in their own catechisms.

📖 Searching Scripture

1. It is reported that three times Dominic raised the dead to life. Find at least three incidents in the Bible where Jesus raised the dead to life.
2. In addition to performing miracles and possessing the gift of prophecy (He predicted the date of his own death.), Dominic was possessed the gift of tongues. Read about the various gifts of the Holy Spirit in 1 Corinthians 12:4-11.

Book Summary Test for *Saint Dominic*

Directions: Answer in complete sentences. If necessary, use the back of the page for additional writing space. 100 possible points, 20 points for each answer.

1. In what century did St. Dominic live? In what countries did he spend most of his life?

   _____

   _____

   _____

2. Name the two prayers that St. Dominic de Guzman prayed most constantly.

   _____

   _____

3. To whom did St. Dominic have a special devotion?

   _____

   _____

4. What was the mission of the order Dominic founded? Give at least two names for this order.

   _____

   _____

   _____

   _____

5. St. Dominic took the gift of preaching that God had given him and used it for the salvation of souls. Discuss what gift you possess that, if utilized solely for the glory of God, may be the key to others' sanctity as well as your own.

   _____

   _____

   _____

   _____

   _____

Saint Dominic, Preacher of the Rosary and Founder of the Dominican Order

Answer Key to Comprehension Questions

Chapters 1 and 2—In Which Dominic Travels with Bishop Diego and Begins His Work of Preaching to the Heretics

1. Dominic sacrificed not only his books but also his clothes, his furniture, and whatever money he had in order to obtain money and food for the starving citizens of Palencia.
2. Bishop Diego's attitude regarding his desire to become a missionary to the Tartars in eastern Europe is summarized in this quotation from page 3: "Lord, not my will but Thine be done!"
3. Dominic and Bishop Diego traveled to Rome to see Pope Innocent III as Bishop Diego wished to be relieved of his duties in Osma so that he might become a missionary for the Tartars.
4. Dominic and Bishop Diego found the missionaries in Montpellier to be very discouraged with their lack of conversions.

Chapters 3 and 4—In Which Dominic Hears the Blessed Mother Speak in His Heart and Founds a Religious Community for Women

1. In their schools, heretics were teaching children to hate the sacraments, the pope, and much of the doctrine held in the creed. Dominic and the other monks counteracted this by opening schools of their own to teach the children and to give women converts a safe place to stay.
2. Dominic's gift for public speaking made him a logical choice for the post of superior.
3. The 150 Hail Marys of the complete fifteen-mystery rosary borrowed its number from the number of Psalms in the Old Testament.
4. Dominic's missionaries preached not only in the churches but also in the marketplace, in private homes, in castles—wherever a crowd could be gathered.
5. When confronted by the women heretics, Dominic turned in prayer to the Blessed Virgin.
6. The women were finally convinced that Dominic was speaking the Truth after the devil appeared as a fearsome beast that vanished when Dominic ordered him to leave in the name of the one true God.

Chapters 5 and 6—In Which Dominic Continues to Convert the Albigensians during the War and Challenges Them to Kill Him

1. The Albigensian heretic who challenged Pope Innocent III was Count Raymond of Toulouse.
2. Dominic went to Carcassonne as it was a "hotbed of heresy" (page 36) where Catholics were persecuted for their faith. He was willing to die a martyr for Christ. In 1215, Dominic went to Rome with Bishop Foulques to attend an important meeting. There he met Pope Innocent II and Brother Francis of Assisi.
3. In Prouille in mid-April of 1216, sixteen men from various countries—some priests, some clerics not yet ordained, and some laymen—meet for the purpose of establishing a Rule to govern the new Order of Preachers (page 49).

Chapters 7 and 8—In Which Dominic Founds His Order of Monks and Sends Them Out to Establish Convents

1. The second vision that Dominic received while at the Basilica of St. Peter was of Sts. Peter and Paul presenting him with a pilgrim's staff and a book of the Gospels. "Go and preach, for to this work you are called," they told him (page 53).
2. After giving his blessing for Dominic's new order of monks, Pope Honorius III bestowed upon Dominic the honor of his request to preach at the churches of Rome.
3. In addition to his monastery in Toulouse, France, Dominic also established convents in Paris, France, and Madrid, Spain.
4. When he became overwhelmed with his new responsibilities, Brother Stephen asked Dominic to remember him in prayer.

5. According to Dominic, the most valuable gift anyone has ever given us is the gift of salvation—the chance to go to heaven when we die. It is our free will cooperating with God's grace.

Chapters 9 and 10—In Which Reginald Joins the Friars, and Dominic Performs Miracles

1. After giving the monastery of St. Sixtus to Dominic in 1218, Pope Honorius III asked Dominic to organize the various communities of nuns living in Rome into one body.
2. Reginald was making a pilgrimage to the Holy Land in order to find peace with his lifestyle.
3. The "secret" to Dominic's success as a preacher was his zeal for souls; he had been offering himself to God for the salvation of souls since he was a child.
4. When Mary replaced the linen surplice of Dominic's habit with the white woolen scapular, she gave the title of "The Brothers of Mary" to Dominic's monks.
5. When food was short in Dominic's community, angels would come at mealtime with freshly baked loaves of bread.

Chapters 11 and 12—In Which Brother Reginald Gathers More Souls at Bologna, and We Learn the Story of Blessed Diana

1. After the angels' second visit to the monastery with the loaves of bread, the friars henceforth served the lay brothers and novices first at mealtime.
2. In an attempt to increase the number of people coming to hear him preach in the church of St. Mary of Mascarella, Brother Reginald told the people about the Blessed Virgin and the rosary.
3. Brother Reginald was compared to St. Paul and the prophet Elias due to the eloquence and persuasiveness of his preaching.
4. In order to show her appreciation for Brother Reginald's counsel, Diana arranged to have her grandfather allow the friars the use of the Church of St. Nicholas and its adjoining land for a monastery. This property had been in her family for generations.
5. As Diana recited her vows to God, Dominic foresaw the sufferings of Diana in her religious life—her struggles with her family, her physical sufferings, and her role in establishing the order's house for women in Bologna.

Chapters 13 and 14—In Which Dominic Organizes the Nuns' Communities of Rome and Raises Napoleon Orsini from the Dead

1. Holiness depends, in a large measure, upon our willingness to suffer.
2. Two years prior, Honorius III, upon giving the Church of St. Sixtus to Dominic, had requested him to unite the various communities of nuns in Rome to live under one rule similar to the rule of poverty, study, and prayer that Dominic had established in Prouille.
3. Mother Eugenia from St. Mary's did not want to move her community of nuns to St. Sixtus because they were the custodians of a picture of the Blessed Virgin painted by St. Luke, which she felt should stay at the convent of St. Mary's.
4. The sisters of St. Mary's were convinced to move to St. Sixtus and adopt the rule prepared by Dominic by Dominic himself. His prayers and penances for them prepared the way, while the inspiration of the Holy Spirit convinced them of the emptiness of their lives.
5. Dominic attributes true happiness in this life to the willing acceptance of suffering.
6. Many consider the nuns' acceptance of Dominic's Rule a miracle. Also reported in this chapter is the miraculous elevation of Dominic while praying at Mass and the rising of Napoleon Orsini from the dead by Dominic's praying the Sign of the Cross over him.

Chapters 15 and 16—In Which Hyacinth and His Companions Join Dominic's Order, and We Learn of Dominic's Youth

1. Dominic felt that Brother Jordan would succeed him as head of the Order of Preachers.Bishop Ivo Odrowatz of Cracow asked Dominic to send some of his friars to Poland to reach. Instead, Dominic trained the bishop's two nephews and two of his servants to evangelize Poland as friars of the Order of Preachers.

2. The mission of Dominic's order was to convert the leaders of the heretics by men who are gifted in learning. Dominic was told in a vision by Sts. Peter and Paul, "Go, and preach, for to this work you are called" (page 53). In the thirteenth century, this was a new kind of religious order—to preach the Gospel. Now Dominic's order is known simply as the "Dominicans" rather than their original name of the "Order of the Preachers" but preaching remains their special mission and duty. (Now you know when you see the initials "O.P." after a name that they belong to the Dominican order.)

3. Dominic told Bishop Ivo that the best possible gift we can give each other is to remember each other in prayer.

4. Dominic's two brothers were Anthony, who was a parish priest in Spain, and Mannes, who was a member of the Dominican order and chaplain for the sisters in their convent at Prouille, France.

Chapters 17 and 18—In Which Dominic Establishes the Secular Third Order of Dominicans and Dies a Holy Death

1. The "Militia of Jesus Christ" is the name Dominic gave to the group of zealous laymen who offered themselves for the defense of the Church. They wore white tunics and black mantles with the black and white cross of the Order of Preachers. They were to recite certain prayers each day and would share in the good works of the entire Order while remaining at home.

2. Dominic adopted the two mottoes of *Laudare, benedicere, praedicare*, which means "To praise, to bless, to preach"; and *Veritas*, which means "truth."

3. Dominic wished to die at the monastery of St. Nicolas and be buried there "at the feet of my brethren" (page 152).

Answer Key to Book Summary Test

1. St. Dominic was born in 1170 and died in 1221 so he lived in both the twelfth and thirteenth centuries. He spent the majority of his preaching life in France and Italy.

2. St. Dominic's two favorite prayers were the Sign of the Cross and the Hail Mary.

3. St. Dominic had a special devotion to the Blessed Virgin Mary.

4. The special mission of St. Dominic's order was preaching and teaching. His order was known as the Order of Preachers, the Friars Preachers, the Black Friars, and also the Brothers of Mary. Today they usually are referred to simply as Dominicans.

5. Answers will vary.

Study Guide for

The Children of Fatima and Our Lady's Message to the World

The Children of Fatima

Three children from Fatima were tending their sheep.
A visit from an angel the children did reap.
He visited them thrice—
Taught them sacrifice.
Their promise to suffer and pray they did keep.

The intent of the angel was to prepare
For the Lady's coming and make them aware
Of the need to pray
And always obey—
Do penance, make sacrifice, remember prayer.

The mother of Jesus came to them five times
She came without bells, without whistles or chimes.
She asked them to pray
The Rosary each day
And showed them where sinners were put for their crimes.

A vision was shown them, a vision of hell.
Three secrets were shown; they promised not to tell.
In spite of the threats,
They had no regrets.
A miracle she'd show before her farewell.

They fasted, they prayed, did all that she asked.
Though all were quite young, they handled the task.
The miracle was done
Making use of the sun.
Though wet from the rain in the sun they did bask.

Soon after, our Lady took two home again
While on earth here Lucia for us did remain.
To keep us from sinning—
The devil from winning—
And devotion to her heart from us to obtain.

Think what you can learn from the children and their tale.
How you can apply it to help you prevail.
Then mold what you do
And boldly pursue
Their pattern of holiness. Follow their trail.

Timeline of World War I Events

Year	Event
06/28/**1914**	Archduke Francis Ferdinand of Austria assassinated at Sarajevo
07/28; 08/04	Austria-Hungary declares war on Serbia; Germany invades Belgium
9/5-9/10; 9/11	First Battle of the Marne; Germans end retreat at Aisne River line
10/10	Antwerp surrendered
10/19-11/21	First Battle of Ypres
02/18/**1915**	Germans begin submarine blockade of British Isles
04/22-05/25	Second Battle of Ypres; first use of poison gas in warfare
04/25; 05/07	British land in Gallipoli; Steamship Lusitania sank off Irish coast
June - September	Russians driven back on Eastern Front
10/03-10/05	Allied forces land at Salonika
1/07-1/08/**1916**	British withdraw from Gallipoli
02/21-09/3	Series of battles in Verdun area; Germans finally driven back
Spring 1916	Approximate time of the first apparition of the Angel
05/31	Battle of Jutland
07/01-07/13	Battle of Somme
Summer 1916	Approximate time of the second apparition of the Angel
07/14-09/03	Second Battle of Somme
Fall 1916	Approximate time of the third apparition of the Angel
12/06	Germans capture Bucharest
02/01/**1917**	Germany begins unrestricted submarine warfare
03/15	Revolution forces Czar Nicholas of Russia to give up his throne
05/13; 06/13	First apparition of our Lady; second apparition of our Lady
06/25	First United States troops land in France
07/13	Third apparition of our Lady
07/31-11/10	Third Battle of Ypres
8/19; 9/13	Fourth apparition of our Lady; fifth apparition of our Lady
10/13	Sixth apparition of our Lady—Miracle of the Sun
10/24-12/26	Italians defeated at Caporetto and driven back
11/07	Bolsheviks seize control of Russia
11/20-12/03; 12/09	Battle of Cambrai; British capture Jerusalem
12/17	Russian armistice with Germany
01/08/**1918**	President Wilson announces Fourteen Points
03/03	Russian signs Treaty of Brest-Litovsk
03/21-04/16	Third Battle of Somme
05/27-06/06	Third Battle of Aisne
06/06-06/25	Battle of Belleau Wood
07/21	Allies recapture Chateau Thierry
09/12-09/16	Battle of St. Mihiel
09/26; 09/29	Battle of Meuse-Argonne begins German retreat; Bulgaria surrenders
10/30	Turkey accepts armistice terms
11/01-11/04	Hungary and Austria become separate republics; Austria accepts armistice
11/07-11/09	Revolution begins in Germany; Kaiser William II abdicates
11/11	Germans sign armistice
04/04/1919	Francisco Marto dies of influenza
06/28	Treaty of Versailles signed
02/20/1920	Jacinta Marto dies after more than a year of suffering
2/13/2005	Death of Lucia Dos Santos, Carmelite nun, at the age of 97

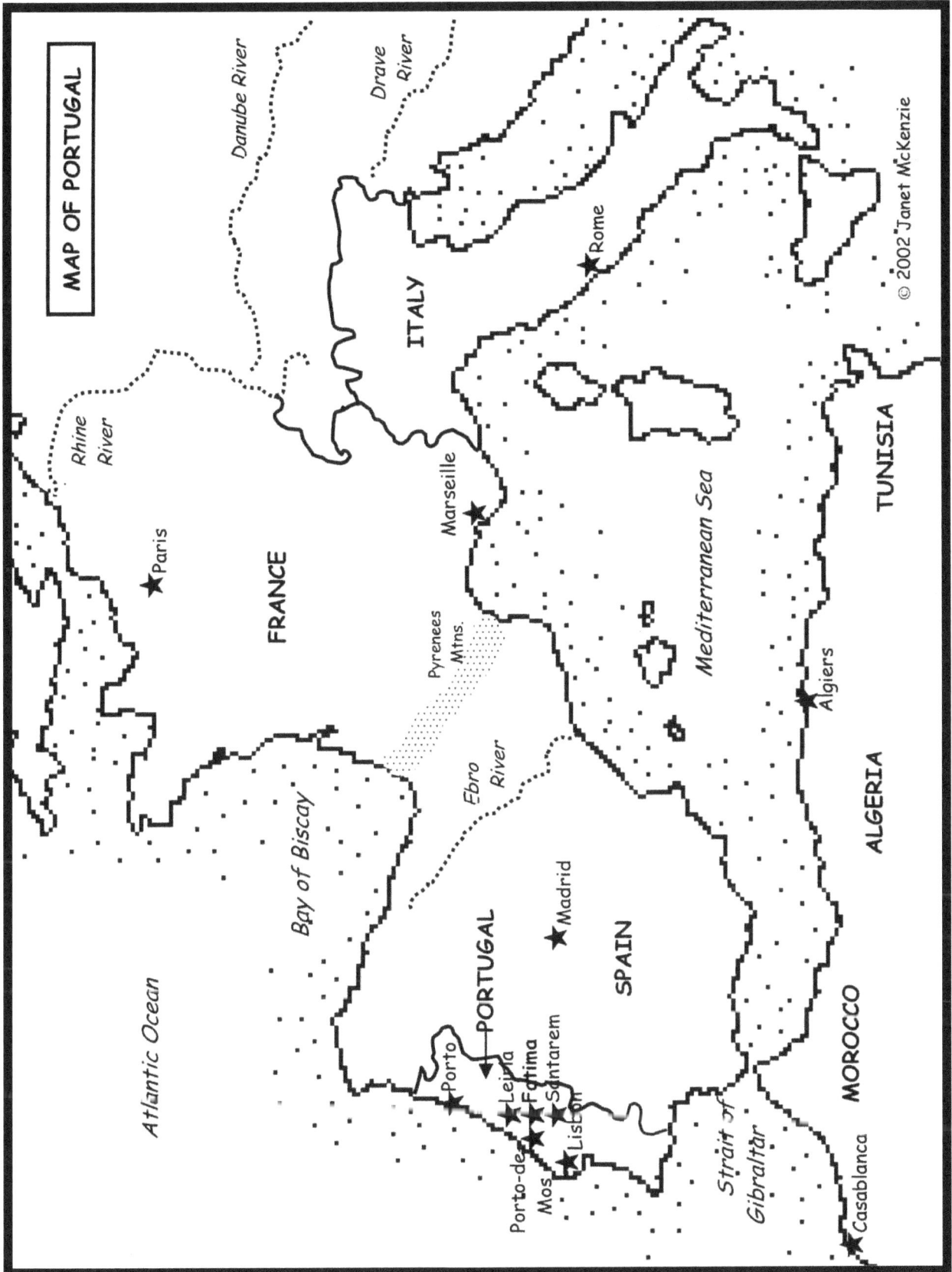

MAP OF PORTUGAL

Danube River

Drave River

© 2002 Janet McKenzie

Rhine River

ITALY

Rome

Paris

FRANCE

Marseille

Mediterranean Sea

TUNISIA

Pyrenees Mtns.

Ebro River

Algiers

Bay of Biscay

ALGERIA

Atlantic Ocean

Madrid

SPAIN

PORTUGAL

Porto

Leiria

Fatima

Santarem

MOROCCO

Porto-de-

Mos

Lisbon

Strait of Gibraltar

Casablanca

Chapter 1–In Which the Angel of Peace Teaches the Children to Pray

---

✞REVIEW✞ Vocabulary

he was little *inclined*   *Host*
in this *sublime* prayer   *chalice*

??? Comprehension Questions/Narration Prompts

1. State the names and ages of each of the children who were present for the appearances of the angel at Fatima.
2. Name some of the things the children did for amusement as they watched their parents' sheep each day.
3. What was Francisco's attitude toward the rosary and church?
4. How many times did the angel appear to the children? State the times and give a brief summary of each visit.

Forming Opinions/Drawing Conclusions

Jacinta and Francisco were surprised to have the angel offer Communion to them as "they knew only a very little of the catechism!" (page 7). Consider the following statement from the *Decree on First Communion* as issued by Pope Pius X on August 8, 1910: "A full and perfect knowledge of Christian doctrine is not necessary either for First Confession or for First Communion. Afterwards, however, the child will be obliged to learn gradually the entire Catechism according to his ability. The knowledge of religion which is required in a child in order to be properly prepared to receive First Communion is such that he will understand according to his capacity those Mysteries of faith which are necessary as a means of salvation and that he can distinguish between the Bread of the Eucharist and ordinary, material bread, and thus he may receive Holy Communion with a devotion becoming his years." What knowledge was required of Jacinta and Francisco that they may properly receive Communion? Discuss whether all three children received Communion equally—did all three truly receive the Body, Blood, Soul, and Divinity of Jesus? (See the answer key for another instance of an angel administering Holy Communion.)

✞ Growing in Holiness

Memorize both prayers taught to the shepherd children. Recite these prayers daily three times each with your head bowed to the ground or floor as the angel did. These prayers help us make reparation for our sins and the sins of all mankind; pray them often to help fulfill the requests of Our Lady of Fatima.

Geography

Trace the map of Portugal found on page 23 of this guide. Label and color the seas and rivers blue. This map will be completed in Chapter 8.

Chapter 2–In Which Our Lady Visits the Shepherd Children

🔳REVIEW🔳Vocabulary

an *exquisite* rosary of white pearls   *convert*
a small *holm-oak* tree   *reparation*

⁇⁇⁇ Comprehension Questions/Narration Prompts

1. When was the first appearance of our Lady to the shepherd children?
2. Who heard and spoke to our Lady?
3. Why did the children want to keep the visit of the lady a secret?

💡 Forming Opinions/Drawing Conclusions

When Francisco asked Lucia how making small sacrifices can convert sinners, she replied, "Don't ask questions. The Angel told us what to do, and we should obey him" (page 11). How would you answer Francisco's question?

📖 For Further Study

Jacinta states that they were hoping for an end to the war soon (page 10). She is referring to the First World War, which started on June 28, 1914, and ended on June 28, 1919. Research this war. Be sure to look up the causes of the war and the countries most severely affected by the war. Who were the main political characters involved? What were the major battles? What caused the war's end? Use the timeline provided on page 22 of this study guide to help you.

🖼 Timeline Work

Taping sheets of plain paper end-to-end, make a timeline representing the years from 1914 to 1919. Let three inches equal 25 years. Mark on your timeline the dates and events from 1914 to the fall of 1916 as found on page 22 of this study guide.

✝ Growing in Holiness

Our Lady stated that the young girl Amelia will be in Purgatory until the end of the world (page 13). Recite the following "Prayer for Daily Neglects" from a nun who appeared shortly after her death to her Abbess and told her, "I went straight to Heaven, for, by means of this prayer recited every evening, I paid all my debts."

> Eternal Father, I offer Thee the Sacred Heart of Jesus, with all its love, all its sufferings, and all its merits. First—To expiate all the sins I have committed this day and during all my life, (Recite one Glory Be). Second—To purify the good I have done poorly this day and during all my life, (Recite one Glory Be). Third—To supply for the good I ought to have done, and that I have neglected this day and all my life, (Recite one Glory Be). Amen.

Chapter 3–In Which the Our Lady Gives the Children Another Prayer and Promises to Take Jacinta and Francisco to Heaven Soon

___

✖REVIEW✖Vocabulary

news was being *imparted*   *apparition*
shepherds paid *scant* attention   *Immaculate Heart*

??? Comprehension Questions/Narration Prompts

1. How did the children's parents and the priest react when told of our Lady's visit?
2. What did Father Ferreira advise the children's mothers to do?
3. How many people were present at our Lady's visit on June 13, 1917? What was the first part of her message to the children in this visit?

For Further Study

Research briefly the life of St. Anthony of Padua, who was born in Lisbon, Portugal, in 1195 and died in Padua in 1231; and the life of St. John Eudes, born in France in 1601 and died in 1680. What are they known for? What/who are they the patron saints of? When are their feast days?

✝ Growing in Holiness

Memorize the Fatima Prayer (also called the "Decade Prayer") that our Lady taught the children. Remember to add this prayer after each Glory Be of the rosary.

Timeline Work

Make a copy of the chart on page 28 of this study guide. Write a summary of the messages of the angel's appearances and the first message of our Lady. Add a summary of each appearance of our Lady after the event occurs in the text. Complete this activity as though our Lady was appearing to you. What does Our Lady of Fatima request of you?

✓ Checking the Catechism

The children's parents believed the parish priest to be a representative of Christ. Study the Church's teachings on the priesthood. Older students may read the following text paragraphs from the *Catechism of the Catholic Church (CCC)*: 1142, 1548, 1551, 1563-66, 1577-78, and 1581-83 (322-336) while younger students study this topic in their catechisms. If desired, complete Activity #54 in *100 Activities Based on the Catechism of the Catholic Church (100 Activities)*.

Searching Scripture

Read the following scriptural passages relating to hell: Matthew 13:36-43, Matthew 25:30 and 41; 2 Thessalonians 1:5-10; and Revelation (Apocalypse) 19:20. Make notes on these citations as they will be needed in Chapter 5.

Timeline of Fatima Events

Date	Message
Spring 1916	
Mid-summer 1916	
Fall 1916	
May 13, 1917	
June 13, 1917	
July 13, 1917	
August 19, 1917	
September 13, 1917	
October 13, 1917	

Chapter 4–In Which Our Lady Continues the Message of Her Second Visit

---

⟨REVIEW⟩ Vocabulary

Immaculate Heart will be your *refuge*   *blasphemies*
pointed *resolutely* to the small holm-oak   *Gloria*

?? Comprehension Questions/Narration Prompts

1. What happened when our Lady stretched out her hands toward the children?
2. What devotion did our Lady request in order to make her Heart known and loved by others? What promises did she attach to this devotion?
3. What sign allowed some of the onlookers at the second visit to believe that the lady had actually been at the holm-oak?

Forming Opinions/Drawing Conclusions

1. Explain what is necessary to meet the conditions of the First Five Saturdays—an offering made by us to console Mary's Immaculate Heart. How will this devotion help to make the Immaculate Heart of Mary better known and loved?
2. On page 35, the peasant woman points out that the leaves on the holm-oak had been bent by the lady's visit. If you have been there, would this evidence have helped you believe that the messages were truly from heaven? Discuss the relationship between faith and evidence (reason).

✝ Growing in Holiness

1. Begin to pray each day before the crucifix. Make the Sign of the Cross reverently; St. Dominic often used this prayer alone to invoke God's miraculous assistance. If necessary, use a spiritual book to prevent distractions, but remember that St. Thomas Aquinas said that the finest book of all is the crucifix.
2. If you have not yet made the First Saturday Communions of Reparation, begin to attend Mass on the first Saturday of each month in addition to completing the other requirements. Make this lifetime devotion even if all Saturdays are not consecutive.

✓ Checking the Catechism

1. Part of the fulfillment of the First Five Saturdays involves the recitation of the rosary and meditation upon the mysteries of the rosary. If you do not yet have the twenty mysteries memorized, do so now. Older students should read about the rosary in the CCC in text paragraphs 971, 1674, 2678, and 2708 (198, 353, 563, 567, and 570) while younger students study this topic in their own catechisms. If desired, complete Activities #68 and #69 in *100 Activities*.
2. Our Lady asked the children to "pray, to pray much" (page 34). Read what the *CCC* teaches on this subject by reading text paragraphs 2559-65, 2700-2708, 2729-37 and 2752-58 (535, 567, and 572-576).

Chapter 5–In Which the Children Receive Three Secrets from Our Lady and Experience a Vision of Hell

✦REVIEW✦Vocabulary

persecutions of the church   *consecration*
people . . . were *milling* about   *dogma*

??? Comprehension Questions/Narration Prompts

1. How many people attended the expected third visit of Our Lady of Fatima on July 13, 1917? Compare this with the previous month's attendance.
2. What are the three secrets of this message from our Lady?
3. Describe how Lucia's life at home has changed since the first visit of our Lady.

Forming Opinions/Drawing Conclusions

1. Using the notes taken in Chapter 3, compare Holy Scripture's description of hell with what the children saw during this vision. How do you think reading about hell and knowing of its existence is different from actually seeing a vision of it?
2. Discuss the "new life" that the children of Fatima experienced after the third vision in July. Explain the change in their attitudes as well as their general spiritual conversions. (Older students may read in the *CCC* text paragraph 1848.) List some ways to imitate the children of Fatima—"little sacrifices that no one will notice" (page 43).

✝ Growing in Holiness

The children of Fatima are now praying with joy and peace. The rays of grace given to them by the Blessed Virgin have changed their prayer lives. Ask daily for this grace. When our Lady appeared to St. Catherine Laboure of France in 1830, she talked about the graces and blessings that flow out of the rays of her hands. But so many do not ask for these graces! Be sure to ask our Lady for the grace to want to pray, not from a sense of duty but from a true love of God and a longing to convert sinners. (Examine a miraculous medal to see these rays.)

✓ Checking the Catechism

Older students may read text paragraphs 1451-1454 (300 and 303) pertaining to contrition in the *CCC* while younger students study contrition in their own catechisms.

📖 Searching Scripture

Read Matthew 13:54-58. How does this apply to this chapter's contents? Read too the "Psalm of Contrition," Psalm 51 (50), which is also known as the "Miserere" or the "Prayer of Repentance."

Chapter 6–In Which the Mayor Prevents the Children from Meeting with Our Lady

---

✖REVIEW✖ Vocabulary

prominence to Fatima   *prophets*
an evil *scheme* was brewing in his mind   *seminaries*

??? Comprehension Questions/Narration Prompts

1. Why was the mayor of Ourem upset about the events at Fatima?
2. How did Lucia react to the questions of the mayor?
3. What is the scheme of the mayor regarding the children of Fatima?

Forming Opinions/Drawing Conclusions

1. Refute the deputy's idea that religion is only a cleverly organized business that is old-fashioned and not to be tolerated in an up-to-date country. Why is religion still important in a "progressive" world?
2. Placing yourself in the same situation of the three children, discuss what your fears, thoughts, and actions might be at this point in the story.

For Further Study

Research one of the following topics: 1) Communism—especially as it pertains to Leninism and the Bolshevik Revolution in Russia in 1917 or 2) the famous grotto at Lourdes, which became a place of pilgrimage in 1858.

✝ Growing in Holiness

Lucia reveals to the mayor another prayer the children had been given during the July 13th apparition: the "Sacrifice Prayer" as found on page 50 of the Windeatt biography. Memorize this prayer. Recite it often during the day as sacrifices for sinners are made. Pray that a great many sinners will be converted!

✓ Checking the Catechism

Atheists are people who believe that there is no God. Younger students should study the first three Commandments in their catechisms. Older students may read text paragraphs 2123-2128 (445, 447, and 453) in the *CCC*. Complete Activity #18 in *100 Activities*.

📖 Searching Scripture

Read Luke 23:1-15. How do the curiosity and intentions of the mayor of Ourem compare with that of Pilate? In what ways were the circumstances similar and how were they different?

Chapter 7–In Which the Faith and Spiritual Courage of the Children Are Tested

✖REVIEW✖Vocabulary
God's anger . . . might be *appeased*   *medal*
he *fumed*   *Immaculate Heart of Mary*

??? Comprehension Questions/Narration Prompts
1. How did the other prisoners at Ourem react to Lucia, Jacinta, and Francisco?
2. What did the mayor do on the fifth day of the children's imprisonment?
3. What did Lucia do when she thought that Jacinta and Francisco had been killed?

Forming Opinions/Drawing Conclusions
1. All three of the children were willing to die as martyrs rather than reveal the secret the lady had entrusted to them or to deny her existence. If you were in their place, what graces or assistance would you ask from heaven in order to obtain the privilege to die as a martyr for your Faith? Name some small crucifixions you can undergo each day to prepare for possible persecution or martyrdom.
2. What effect, if any, do you think the children's actions had on their fellow prisoners? What effect did they have on the mayor? Do you think any of these people changed their ideas about or relationship with God because of the children? Why do some people have so much faith in God and others so little? What can you do to help your faith (or someone else's) grow today?

For Further Study
Read the following passages: Matthew 10:16-20, Luke 12:4-5, Acts 7:51-60 (59), Acts 16:25-40, and Acts 21:13-14. Also read these text paragraphs from the *CCC*: 852 (173) and 2473-74 (522). Write a report to summarize these readings, relating them to the events in this chapter as well as to our need to be prepared to die for our Faith.

✚ Growing in Holiness
Jacinta, even in prison, prays the rosary as our Lady had requested. She prays it on her knees with her hands folded. How often do you pray on your knees in humble submission to God? Remember the importance of posture when you pray—not only with your daily rosary but also with your morning and night prayers.

✓ Checking the Catechism
Older students may read further in the *CCC* text paragraphs 1667-79 (351) on sacramentals of the Church. Younger children should be asked to find sacramentals in their home. Discuss the purpose and use of sacramentals.

Chapter 8–In Which the Events of August 13th Are Told, and Our Lady Makes Her August Visit

---

✶REVIEW✶ Vocabulary

a disgusted mayor was *depositing* them   *scruples*
gazing after her with *rapt* faces   *miracle*

??? Comprehension Questions/Narration Prompts

1. Did the crowd who gathered for the lady's visit on August 13th receive a miracle as they expected?
2. Relate what happened on August 19th while the children were shepherding their sheep near the village of Valinhos.
3. What did our Lady tell Lucia to do with the gifts people were leaving at the holm-oak?

✝ Growing in Holiness

Begin a family tradition of processions on feast days. Carry candles, homemade banners and/or statues. Sing hymns or pray appropriate litanies. Process either room to room in your home or throughout the neighborhood. Perhaps you can begin or end at a church. Celebrate with a special food that day. Don't forget to celebrate each member's baptismal day in this way too.

Geography

Using the map of Portugal started in Chapter 1, label the countries in green and the cities in red. Notice that on the map provided, rivers and seas are in italics, cities are indicated with a star, and countries are in capital letters. Find Portugal—a country slightly larger than the state of Maine—on a globe or world map. (Note that the Cova da Iria is not a village but a large hollow located about a mile from the village of Fatima.)

Timeline Work

If you have not already done so, please add a summary of the June, July, and August visits of our Lady. Be specific regarding what actions and prayers she requested.

✓ Checking the Catechism

". . . the Lady repeated that she was deeply offended by the mayor's actions, that such sinful conduct must be punished and that all Portugal must share in the punishment" (page 71). Just as each of our good actions build up the Body of Christ, so does each sin that we commit damage it. Younger students should reference the communion of saints in their catechisms. Older students may read about this doctrine in the *CCC*, text paragraphs 946-962, 1055, 1331, 1474-1477, and 2635 (194-195, 211, and 554).

Chapter 9–In Which Our Lady Gives Her Fifth Message to the Children of Fatima

⟪REVIEW⟫Vocabulary
she was about to *manifest* herself
we should be very *prudent*

Queen of Heaven
Sign of the Cross

??? Comprehension Questions/Narration Prompts
1. How many people were expected for the September apparition as compared with the crowd for the August vision?
2. What was a sign that the lady was approaching?
3. Did all the people present for the fifth visit of our Lady believe that she was truly present?

Forming Opinions/Drawing Conclusions
The apparitions at Fatima were declared "worthy of belief" by the Church in 1930. Defend the actions of the parish priest of Fatima. Why is it important that he (and us as well!) not become too involved in visions and revelations that do not have Church approval?

For Further Study
Research the origin of the rosary as well as the Confraternity of the Rosary. Investigate the lives of the following Catholics and their relationship to the rosary: St. Dominic, Blessed Alan, and St. Louis de Montfort.

Growing in Holiness
Our Lady is said to be "so bright and beautiful that the sun become as nothing in her presence" (page 77). Pray the Litany of the Blessed Virgin (Litany of Loreto). Note especially the following titles appropriate to our study of Our Lady of Fatima: "Gate of Heaven," "Morning Star," and "Queen of the Most Holy Rosary."

✓ Checking the Catechism
Our Lady promised that in October St. Joseph and the Child Jesus would come. Prepare for this by reading about St. Joseph in the *CCC*: 437, 532-34, 1014, 1846, and 2177 (104). Younger students may read about the Incarnation and birth of Jesus in their own catechisms.

Searching Scripture
Read more about St. Joseph in Matthew 1:18-25 and 2:13-23, and Luke 2:41-52.

Chapter 10—In Which the Great Miracle of the Sun Occurs

✴REVIEW✴Vocabulary
raised in honest *supplication*   *graces*
state the various *petitions* given   *scapular*

⁇⁇ Comprehension Questions/Narration Prompts
1. How did the children of Fatima feel about the promised miracle that was to occur on October 13, 1917? How did Lucia's mother feel about it?
2. What was the mission or purpose of the messages given by Our Lady of Fatima?
3. Other than the vision of the Holy Family, who did Lucia see?

For Further Study
Our Lady of Fatima appeared to Lucia as Our Lady of Mount Carmel, wearing the Carmelite habit and carrying a scapular. Research the history of the Carmelite order including the contributions of these saints: Berthold, Simon Stock, John of the Cross, and Teresa of Avila. Read Mary Fabyan Windeatt's coloring book, *The Brown Scapular*.

Growing in Holiness
The miracle of the sun caused many people to believe that the end of the world had come; they pled for mercy and made acts of contrition. Using the Ten Commandments and the beatitudes, make a sincere examination of conscience. Begin to examine your conscience each night, followed by an act of contrition. Make resolutions for the following day, choosing one sinful habit to begin to correct. If it has been more than a month since receiving the Sacrament of Penance, make arrangements to do so this weekend. If you do not yet have an act of contrition memorized, memorize one now.

Timeline Work
Complete your Fatima timeline by adding the September and October messages.

✓ Checking the Catechism
Recitation of the rosary showers graces upon those who recite it and builds up the spiritual treasury of the Church. Study temporal punishment and indulgences in your own catechism, or read text paragraphs 1471-79 and 1498 (263, 310, and 312) in the *CCC*.

Searching Scripture
Read about another solar miracle in Joshua (Josue) 10:12-13, how the Lord appeared to Saul in a light brighter than the sun in Acts 26:13, and how God's glory can give light in Revelation (Apocalypse) 21:23.

Chapter 11–In Which the Children Begin to Live According to the Instructions of Our Lady

Vocabulary
small chance of becoming *conceited*   *mortifications*
said their good mother *placidly*   *superstitious*

Comprehension Questions/Narration Prompts
1. From where was the miracle of the sun seen?
2. List the members of Lucia's family as mentioned on page 100.
3. How many souls did the children see in their vision of hell?

For Further Study
"Upheld by grace, which constantly flooded their hearts because they did not forget to ask the Blessed Mother for the grace to do all that God desired of them, they became true victim souls" (page 105). Read about another victim soul closely associated with the Fatima message: Alexandrina Maria da Costa, who was born in 1904 in Balasar, Portugal. As you read the 120-page book, *Alexandrina, The Agony and the Glory* by Francis Johnston, take notes on the references to Jacinta and the Fatima message. Write a brief paper connecting the victim soul Alexandrina to the Fatima message.

Growing in Holiness
Remembering that the children saw not many souls in hell but "billions and billions," renew your efforts to make sacrifices for sinners as outlined in Chapter 5. As Our Lady of Fatima stated, "Penance! Penance! Penance!" Each day "offer up" some sacrifice for sinners and the Holy Souls of Purgatory. Especially remember to keep Friday as a day of penance; despite some popular misconception, Fridays continue to be days of penance for Catholics. In 1966, the Catholic Bishops of the United States removed the requirement of abstinence from meat on Fridays (except during Lent). Their reasoning was that abstaining from meat may not be the best means of practicing penance. However, at this same time, the bishops gave each of us the responsibility of disciplining ourselves with another more meaningful form of fasting and penance. Just as you keep Sunday a day of celebration in remembrance of Christ's resurrection, make Friday a day of penance in remembrance of His great sacrifice for you.

Timeline Work
Add the dates and events from December 6, 1916 through December 17, 1917 to your World War I timeline.

Chapter 12–In Which the Children Attend School, and Francisco Receives His First Holy Communion

---

✖REVIEW✖Vocabulary

they would have been *dumbfounded*   *feast days*
in constant *requiem*   *Easter duty*

??? Comprehension Questions/Narration Prompts

1. Despite the staring and whispering of the other children, why did the three children want to stay in school?
2. When did the Blessed Virgin appear again to Jacinta and Francisco? What did she say?
3. What was the one thing that troubled Francisco as he neared death?

Forming Opinions/Drawing Conclusions

Describe the change in Francisco's attitude toward the Church, the rosary, visits to the Blessed Sacrament, etc. What caused his attitude to change? Has yours changed?

For Further Study

"But in the late fall of 1918, a terrible plague began sweeping over Europe" (page 113). From 1918 to 1919, Europe and the United States suffered an epidemic of influenza. Research "influenza." What are its causes and symptoms? Is it still a dangerous disease?

Growing in Holiness

Francisco no longer feels that the rosary is a tiresome repetition of prayers. Now with his soul's eye, he views the mysteries as pictures of the life of our Lord and the Blessed Virgin. Many rosary meditation books contain pictures to illustrate each mystery. Purchase or borrow several of these to enrich your rosary recitation. Re-read Francisco's method of meditation (pages 111-12); try to incorporate this method into your own daily rosary recitation.

✓ Checking the Catechism

". . . their only trips to the village church had been on Sundays and feast days to attend Mass" (page 109). Younger students should study the holy days of obligation while older students read text paragraphs 2168-88 (453-454) in the CCC. Complete Activity #86 in *100 Activities*.

Searching Scripture

Research the Bible to find the five joyful mysteries as outlined on page 112.

Chapter 13–In Which Jacinta's Suffering Increases

✖REVIEW✖ Vocabulary
a severe form of *pleurisy*   *eternity*
An *abcess* had formed in her side   *penance*

??? Comprehension Questions/Narration Prompts
1. On what day did Francisco Martos die?
2. Into whose keeping has our Lord entrusted the peace of the world?

💡 Forming Opinions/Drawing Conclusions
1. What is "The Great Sacrifice"? Does it involve Jacinta or Lucia?
2. Describe in your own words what the "grace of loving souls" is. How does Jacinta demonstrate that grace? How can you demonstrate that grace?

📖 For Further Study
"Tell everyone that God grants graces through the Immaculate Heart of Mary and that they mustn't be shy about asking for them" (page 122). In the *CCC*, study the definition of "Mediator/Mediatrix" in the back Glossary. Then read the following text paragraphs: 618, 967-70, and 1544 (197 and 324) on this topic.

✝ Growing in Holiness
Note the change in the Sacrifice Prayer with an additional petition praying for the Holy Father (page 129). This was added after Jacinta had a vision of the pope with his head in his hands, weeping.

Two other prayers are offered in this chapter: "My God, I love You because of the graces which You have given me," and "Sweet Heart of Mary, be my salvation." Lucia began praying the first prayer after talking with Rev. Dr. Formigao, her first spiritual director.[1] Father Cruz from Lisbon taught them the second prayer. Jacinta said it often. Memorize both of these prayers. Pray them often.

✓ Checking the Catechism
Jacinta received her first Holy Communion in this chapter. Younger students should study the requirements for the proper reception of the Holy Eucharist. Older students can read corresponding text paragraphs in the *CCC*: 1244, 1355, 1382, 1384-98, 1415-19, 1436, 2042, 2120, and 2181-82 (286-292 and 432). Complete Activity #14 in *100 Activities*.

---

[1] Sister Mary Lucia of the Immaculate Heart, *Fatima in Lucia's Own Words, Sister Lucia's Memoirs* (Fatima, Portugal: Postulation Centre, 1989), p. 108.

Chapter 14–In Which We Learn of Jacinta's Love for Sinners As She Continues to Suffer and Make Sacrifices

✖️REVIEW✖️Vocabulary

Jacinta smiled *wanly*   *chastity*
had *recourse* instead to an institution   *Holy Father*

❓❓❓ Comprehension Questions/Narration Prompts

1. Why did Jacinta go to Ourem? What was the result?
2. When and why did Jacinta go to Lisbon?
3. What two privileges did Jacinta describe as "heaven on earth" (page 137)?
4. What was Jacinta's last sacrifice?

💡 Forming Opinions/Drawing Conclusions

Expand on these quotations of Jacinta[2] as recorded at the orphanage by Sister Mary of the Purification:

1. "More souls go to Hell because of sins of the flesh than for any other reason."
2. Many marriages are not good; they do not please our Lord and are not of God!"
3. People are lost because they do not think of the death of our Lord and do not do penance."
4. "If men only knew what eternity is, they would do everything in their power to change their lives."

✝️ Growing in Holiness

"The sins which cause most people to go to hell are the sins against purity" (page 139). Examine different aspects of your life (music, television, dress, reading material, companions, etc.) to determine what adjustments may be needed in your entertainment, bedroom décor, and clothing style. Ask your angel to protect your thoughts. Pray often "Come, Holy Spirit, come" for the strength and perseverance to live a pure life.

✓ Checking the Catechism

Older students may read text paragraphs 1450-60 and 1468-1470 (300-301 and 303) in the *CCC* on contrition and penance, while younger students reference these topics in their catechisms.

📖 Searching Scripture

Read 2 Corinthians 4:16-18 and 1 Peter 4:1-2.

---

[2] Ann Ball, *Modern Saints, Their Lives and Faces, Book Two,* (Rockford, Illinois: Tan Books and Publishers, 1990), p. 301.

Chapter 15–In Which Lucia Leaves Fatima

REVIEW Vocabulary

a *devout* nobleman   *devotion*
public *subscription* had built a . . . chapel   *diocese*

??? Comprehension Questions/Narration Prompts

1. When did Jacinta die and where was she originally buried?
2. After the death of Jacinta, what other trial did Lucia undergo?
3. Where did Lucia go in the spring of 1921 and why?
4. What was to be Lucia's new name?

For Further Study

". . . the Devil had insinuated into the minds of his co-workers on earth the confidence to reject these events as superstitions" (page 145). What is superstition? Which commandment forbids this? Older students can reference this in the *CCC* in text paragraphs 2110-11 and 2138 (445). List several superstitions commonly practiced in American life.

Growing in Holiness

"Somehow the various visits with our Lady, the many prayers and sacrifices she had made for sinners during the past four years, had disposed her soul for the great grace of being completely abandoned to God's Will" (page 150). "Because once again she had asked for and been given the grace to do not her will, but the Will of God" (page 152). Try to abandon yourself to the Will of God; remember that God is with each of us each moment—loving, leading, calling. The time to surrender is now. Begin to practice the presence of God. Do you will what God wills?

Timeline Work

Complete your World War I timeline by adding the dates and events from January 8, 1918 through February 20, 1920.

✓ Checking the Catechism

Baron d'Alvayazer felt that great graces would be showered upon his family if he honored the body of Jacinta (page 144). Review the Church's teachings on honoring saints, relics, and images by reading text paragraphs 828, 1159-62, 1195, and 2683 (240, 242, 264, 429, 446, and 546) in the *CCC*. In their own catechisms, younger students should study these same topics.

✎ Book Summary Test for *The Children of Fatima*

Directions: Answer in complete sentences. If necessary, use the back of the page for additional writing space. 100 possible points, 20 points for each answer.

1. What are the names of the three children of Fatima? How old were they when Our Lady of Fatima first visited them? How were the children of Fatima prepared for the visits of our Lady?

    _____

    _____

    _____

    _____

2. Summarize the messages our Lady gave at Fatima. You may use the chart you completed to help you. Other than praying the specific prayers as given by Our Lady of Fatima and offering sacrifices for sinners, tell how you can fulfill the wishes of Our Lady of Fatima.

    _____

    _____

    _____

3. What was the great miracle that occurred with our Lady's visit on October 13, 1917?

    _____

    _____

4. Briefly tell what happened to each of the three children after the apparitions.

    _____

    _____

5. If you had been given the choice, would you have preferred to be one of the visionaries who died or the one who lived to spread the message? Explain your answer.

    _____

    _____

The Children of Fatima, and Our Lady's Message to the World
Answer Key to Comprehension Questions

Chapter 1—In Which the Angel of Peace Teaches the Children to Pray

1. Three children were present during the appearances of the angel: six-year-old Jacinta Marto; her brother Francisco, who was eight; and their cousin Lucia dos Santos, aged nine.
2. As they watched their parents' sheep each day, the children amused themselves by talking, playing in a nearby cave, playing the "echo game," building houses out of stones or playing in the fields with the sheep. They always made time for the rosary after lunch—a shortened version of it at least.
3. Francisco did not like reciting the rosary or going to church; he felt such things were only for women and girls.
4. Between the spring and fall of 1916, the angel appeared to the children three times, teaching them two prayers to recite and asking them to offer prayers and sacrifices to the Most High. In the spring of 1916, the angel appeared identifying himself as the "Angel of Peace"; he taught them a prayer to be prayed with their foreheads touching the ground. In mid-summer, he again appeared, identifying himself as the "Angel of Portugal"—its Angel Guardian. He asked them to pray continually and instructed them to offer sacrifices as reparation to God. In the fall of 1916, the angel again appeared to the three shepherd children to teach them another prayer to recite. At this time, he also gave them Holy Communion.

Forming Opinions/Drawing Conclusions

St. Faustina reports in her diary, *Divine Mercy in My Soul*, of receiving Holy Communion from an angel in April of 1938 while she was confined to a sanitarium: "Jesus said to me, **Be at peace; I am with you.** Tired, I fell asleep. In the evening, the sister (Sister David) who was to look after me came and said, 'Tomorrow you will not receive the Lord Jesus, Sister, because you are very tired; later on, we shall see.' This hurt me very much, but I said with great calmness, 'Very well,' and, resigning myself totally to the will of the Lord, I tried to sleep. In the morning, I made my meditation and prepared for Holy Communion, even though I was not to receive the Lord Jesus. When my love and desire had reached a high degree, I saw at the bedside a Seraph, who gave me Holy Communion saying these words: 'Behold the Lord of Angels.' When I received the Lord, my spirit was drowned in the love of God and in amazement. This was repeated for thirteen days, although I was never sure he would bring me Holy Communion the next day. Yet, I put my trust completely in the goodness of God, but did not even dare to think that I would receive Holy Communion in this way on the following day.

The Seraph was surrounded by a great light, the divinity and love of God being reflected in him. He wore a golden robe and, over it, a transparent surplice and a transparent stole. The chalice was crystal, covered with a transparent veil. As soon as he gave me the Lord, he disappeared.

Once, when a certain doubt rose within me shortly before Holy Communion, the Seraph with the Lord Jesus stood before me again. I asked the Lord Jesus, and not receiving an answer, I said to the Seraph, "Could you perhaps hear my confession?" And he answered me, "No spirit in heaven has that power." And at that moment, the Sacred Host rested on my lips. (Diary, 1676-77)

Chapter 2 In Which Our Lady Visits the Shepherd Children

1. Our Lady first appeared to the shepherd children on May 13, 1917, slightly more than a year after the Angel's first visit.
2. While Lucia and Jacinta both heard and saw our Lady, only Lucia spoke with her; Francisco was able to see our Lady but could not hear the words she spoke.
3. The children agreed to keep the visit of the lady a secret because they did not feel anyone would believe them. "Alas for the cherished secret!" (page 16).

Chapter 3—In Which Our Lady Gives the Children Another Prayer and Promises to Take Jacinta and Francisco to Heaven Soon

1. Both mothers were very angry, as they did not believe the children. They took the children to the parish priest, as they were unable to get the children to admit that they were telling a lie. The priest, Father Ferreira, felt that the children had imagined the vision as he did not believe they would deliberately lie.
2. Father Ferreira advised the children's mothers not to punish them anymore.
3. Around seventy people gathered in the sheep pasture on June 13, 1917, in anticipation of our Lady's visit to the children. Our Lady asked the children to continue to pray and make sacrifices for sinners and taught them a prayer to add to the rosary after each Glory Be. She told Lucia that she wanted her to learn to read as she would stay for some time on earth, while she would take Jacinta and Francisco to heaven with her soon.

Chapter 4—In Which Our Lady Continues the Message of Her Second Visit

1. When our Lady stretched out her hands toward the children, rays of light extended from the Lady's hands to their hearts, bringing a love and warmth they had never known before.
2. Our Lady requested the devotion of the Five First Saturdays to make her Heart known and loved by others. Attached to this devotion is Mary's promise to assist, at the hour of death, with all graces necessary for that soul to obtain salvation.
3. Some of the onlookers at the second visit began to believe that the lady had actually been at the holm-oak as they had observed the tree prior to the visit; they noticed after the lady's visit that the top branches of the tree had been bent to the east.

Chapter 5—In Which the Children Receive Three Secrets from Our Lady and Experience a Vision of Hell

1. Approximately five thousand people attended the expected third visit of our Lady to the children of Fatima on July 13, 1917. This is compared with seventy people who had attended in June.
2. The first secret of this message was the vision of hell; the second secret involved devotion to the Blessed Virgin and the consecration of Russia. (Lucia revealed both of these visions in 1927; the third secret, regarding the vision of the bishop/pope, was not revealed until May 13, 2000.)
3. Lucia's life at home changed considerably in the months following the first visit of our Lady. Her mother, concerned about the gossip regarding Lucia and the entire dos Santos family, had begun to beat and scold Lucia hoping she would confess her "lie." Lucia's sisters and brother felt she was bringing disgrace upon the family; people would whisper and point as they walked by giving them no peace. Lucia herself was questioned at all times and places by many who wanted to speak with her regarding the visits and messages.

Chapter 6—In Which the Mayor Prevents the Children from Meeting with Our Lady

1. The mayor of Ourem was upset about the events at Fatima as he did not believe in God and did not understand the events taking place. In addition, he was responsible for keeping peace in the territory surrounding Fatima; he felt the apparitions might cause a disturbance.
2. Lucia's reaction to the questions of the mayor was calm, respectful, and firm; she was not intimidated and refused to back down regarding the visions of the lady.
3. As Lucia would not promise not to go to the Cova on August 13th, the mayor developed a scheme to prevent the children from going. He decided to kidnap them.

Chapter 7—In Which the Faith and Spiritual Courage of the Children Are Tested

1. The other prisoners were amazed at the courage of Lucia, Jacinta, and Francisco. They acted respectfully toward them—some in fact even joined in the recitation of the rosary with them.
2. On the fifth day of the children's imprisonment, the mayor's patience with the children ran out. He decided to take drastic measures and told the children that unless they told the "truth" about the Lady, he would boil them alive in oil.

3. When she thought that Jacinta and Francisco had been killed, Lucia stretched out her arms toward heaven and begged our Lady to give her the strength to die as bravely as Jacinta and Francisco did.

Chapter 8—In Which the Events of August 13th Are Told, and Our Lady Makes Her August Visit

1. The crowd who gathered for the lady's visit on August 13th got a miracle: they heard a clap of thunder, and then saw a flash of lightning. The sun began to grow pale and a glowing cloud settled about the little holm-oak and hid it from view. Many more people came to believe that the events of Fatima were supernatural.
2. On August 19th while the children were shepherding their sheep near the village of Valinhos, our Lady appeared to the children. The lady was very displeased with the mayor of Ourem and stated that all Portugal will share in the punishment for his cruelty—the miracle of October 1917 will be much less impressive. She told Lucia what to do with the gifts left by the holm-oak; she again encouraged the children to recite the rosary each day and to continue to make many sacrifices for sinners.
3. Our Lady told Lucia to use some of the gifts to buy stretchers to be used in processions to honor our Lady; the rest were to be used to begin the erection of a chapel in honor of Our Lady of the Rosary.

Chapter 9—In Which Our Lady Gives Her Fifth Message to the Children of Fatima

1. Thirty thousand people were expected for the September apparition as compared to the fifteen thousand who were present for the August vision.
2. Several signs signaled the approach of the lady including a clap of thunder, a bolt of lightning, the dimming of the sun, and the appearance of a small, shining cloud over the holm-oak.
3. Not all the people present for the fifth visit of our Lady believed the apparitions of Fatima were supernatural in nature. Many continued to believe it was a trick performed for attention or money.

Chapter 10—In Which The Great Miracle Of The Sun Occurs

1. At least sixty thousand people were expected to attend the promised miracle that was to occur on October 13, 1917. The children were confident that the lady would come and that the miracle would occur as promised. However, Lucia's mother was worried that all would not go well, and her family would be disgraced.
2. The mission of the messages given by Our Lady of Fatima was to instill in the hearts of not only the three children but also in the hearts of all Catholics a knowledge of the great power of the rosary as well as a willingness to recite this prayer daily.
3. While Jacinta and Francisco shared Lucia's vision of the Holy Family, Lucia herself also enjoyed a vision of our Lord accompanied by His mother as Our Lady of Sorrows. Then our Lady appeared to Lucia as Our Lady of Mount Carmel.

Chapter 11—In Which the Children Begin to Live According to the Instructions of Our Lady

1. The miracle of the sun was seen not only in the Cova da Iria but also throughout all of Portugal.
2. In Lucia's family there were four girls and one boy: Therese, Gloria, Caroline, Lucia, and Manuel.
3. In their description of the vision of hell, the children describe "billions and billions" of condemned souls.

4. ## Chapter 12—In Which the Children Attend School, and Francisco Receives His First Holy Communion

1. Despite the staring and whispering of the other children, the three children wanted to stay in school as it gave them the opportunity to study their catechism and to visit Jesus in the Blessed Sacrament.

2. The Blessed Virgin appeared again to Jacinta and Francisco near the end of October 1918 while they were at home alone. She told them that soon she would take Francisco to heaven but that Jacinta would stay and suffer a while longer.
3. Francisco was troubled by the fact that he had not yet received his First Holy Communion, which he had his heart set upon receiving before his death.

Chapter 13—In Which Jacinta's Suffering Increases
1. Francisco Martos died of influenza on April 4, 1919.
2. Our Lord has entrusted the peace of the world to the Immaculate Heart of Mary.

Chapter 14—In Which We Learn of Jacinta's Love for Sinners as She Continues to Suffer and Make Sacrifices
1. Jacinta went to Ourem at the request of her parents who wished her to undergo treatment for the painful abscess in her side; after two months of regular medical treatment, which was unsuccessful, she was sent home in August of 1919.
2. Jacinta and her mother went to Lisbon in January 1920 so that a specialist could examine Jacinta. In Lisbon she stayed for two weeks at an orphanage before being admitted to the hospital for her surgery, which she had on February 10th.
3. The two privileges Jacinta received at the orphanage that she described as "heaven on earth" were her visits to the Blessed Sacrament and her frequent reception of Holy Communion.
4. Jacinta's last great sacrifice came on the evening before her death when a visiting priest heard her confession but refused to give her Holy Communion as he felt she was not in danger of death.

Chapter 15—In Which Lucia Leaves Fatima
1. After a year a suffering, Jacinta died on February 20, 1920, and was buried in the Baron d'Alvayazer's family vault at Ourem. (However, in 1935, her body was moved to the Fatima cemetery next to Francisco.)
2. In addition to the inability to visit the grave of Jacinta, Lucia also suffered when the atheistic government of Portugal tried to close the Cova da Iria as a place of devotion.
3. On June 17, 1921, at the request of the bishop, Lucia went to the convent boarding school of the Sisters of St. Dorothy at Vilar. The bishop felt that Lucia needed a better school than the one at Fatima as well as some privacy from the constant flow of pilgrims who wanted to see her.
4. The bishop also insisted that Lucia take a new name so no one at the convent would know that she was Lucia, the visionary, to whom the Blessed Virgin had appeared. Her new name was to be Maria das Dores.

Answer Key to Test

1. Jacinta Marto was seven years old when Our Lady of Fatima first appeared to her; her brother Francisco was nine. The third child of Fatima was Lucia dos Santos, who was ten when the apparitions of our Lady first started. The children of Fatima were prepared for the visits of our Lady by the appearance of an angel to them. This occurred three times in the year prior to our Lady's appearance. The angel taught them prayers and asked them to make sacrifices for sinners. On one occasion he gave them Holy Communion.
2. Publicly, the Blessed Virgin appeared to the children six times. She asked them to pray the rosary and make sacrifices every day for the conversion of sinners. She showed them hell where sinners go. She gave them three secrets, which they were not to reveal until our Lady gave them permission to do so. (The rest of answer will vary.)
3. On a rainy day in Fatima, seventy thousand muddy and cold people waited for the miracle. After the appearance of the Lady around noon, the rain stopped. The sun looked like a silver disk which began whirling in the sky shooting off rays of all colors. This lasted for about

three minutes and was repeated two more times. Then the sun appeared to be dashing towards the earth. After some time, it returned to normal, but everyone and everything were miraculously dry.

4. Francisco Marto died on April 4, 1919, of influenza. Jacinta Marto died, after over a year of suffering, on February 20, 1920. (Note that on May 13, 2000, Pope John Paul II beatified both Francisco and Jacinta Marto—the youngest children to receive such an honor. On this same day, he revealed to the world the contents of the "third secret.") Lucia dos Santos left Fatima at the age of fourteen to enter the Sisters of St. Dorothy convent boarding school in Vilar, Portugal. She took her perpetual vows as a Sister of St. Dorothy on October 3, 1934. Due to her need for solitude and seclusion, she desired to become a Discalced Carmelite; she received permission from Pope Pius XII to do so and joined the Carmelite order on March 25, 1948. The Blessed Virgin reportedly appeared to her several times in her adult life. After a long illness, Sister Mary Lucia of the Immaculate Heart died on February 13, 2005, at her Carmelite convent in Coimbra, Portugal, at the age of 97.

5. Answers will vary.

Study Guide for

Saint John Masias, Marvelous Dominican Gatekeeper of Lima, Peru

St. John Masias

When John was quite young, both his mom and dad died.
He went to his uncle who could not provide.
John did not remain
In that part of Spain.
Moved in with a farmer, his sis at his side.

Each day to the fields, he would go with his sheep.
St. John the Evangelist's company did keep.
Never went to school,
But prayer was his tool.
The Holy Souls in Purgatory his merits did reap.

Miraculous travel, he went to Seville.
Then to the Dominicans, God's will to fulfill.
Worked without grumble,
He was too humble
To apply as a priest. His life seemed to stand still.

Fourteen years later, John got a chance
To go to Peru 'cross the ocean's expanse.
With Lima his goal,
And God in control,
A job as a rancher his happy circumstance.

Quit several years later, a lay brother to be—
A Dominican at the monastery.
Worked as a porter,
Obeyed every order,
Provisions to the poor he did oversee.

Sacrificed, prayed, freed souls from their bond,
To John's every prayer God did respond.
Miracles he gained,
Showed how God reigned,
In life and in death, of John all were fond.

Think what you can learn from this saint and his tale.
How you can apply it to help you prevail.
Then mold what you do
And boldly pursue
His pattern of holiness. Follow his trail.

Timeline of Events

Year	Event
1567	City of Rio de Janeiro, Argentina, founded; typhoid fever hits South America
1571	Battle of Lepanto in the Mediterranean Sea–Don Juan defeats the Turks
1579	Martin de Porres born; St. John of the Cross writes "Dark Night of the Soul"
1580	Francis Drake returns to England after sailing around the world
1582	Gregorian Calendar, named for Pope Gregory XIII, adopted by Papal States
1585	Birth of St. John Masias (or Massias) on March 2
1586	Birth of St. Rose in Lima, Peru; the Jesuits found missions in Paraguay
1588	Defeat of the Spanish Armada; Vatican Library opens
1599	Birth of Blessed Marie Guyart of New France; Oliver Cromwell born
1602	Galileo investigates law of gravitation; birth of Blessed Mary of Agreda
1603	Birth of St. Joseph of Cupertino; death of Elizabeth I of England
1605	John travels to Guadalcanar with St. John the Evangelist
1606	Death of Turibius Alphonsus de Mogrovejo on March 23 (born Nov. 16, 1538)
1610	Death of Francis Solano on July 14 in Lima, Peru; first telescope observations made by Galileo; death of King Henry IV of Navarre, France; St. Francis de Sales founds, with St. Jane de Chantal, the Order of Visitation nuns
1617	St. Rose of Lima dies; Pocahontas dies; St. Alphonsus Rodriguez dies
1619	John Masias leaves for South America; first representative assembly in U.S.
1621	Death of St. Robert Bellarmine and St. John Berchmans
1622	John Masias enters the Dominican monastery of Magdalen on January 22; canonization of Francis Xavier, Ignatius Loyola, Philip Neri, and Teresa of Avila
1623	Profession of John Masias as a Dominican lay brother on January 25
1624	John assigned as Gatekeeper or Porter at the convent of Magdalen in Lima; begins the first of his monthly "holidays" on February 10
1626	Rebuilding of St. Peter's Basilica in Rome completed; Francis Bacon dies
1633	Condemnation of Galileo Galilei; outbreak of plague leads to vow of passion play in Oberammergau; Charles I of England is crowned King of Scotland
1639	Death of St. Martin de Porres on November 3; John Masias prophesizes the year of his own death; Rembrandt paints portrait of his mother
1641	Death of St. Jane de Chantal; Catholic rebellion in Ireland
1642	John Masias holds the Christ Child in his arms; death of St. Rene Goupil; capture of St. Isaac Jogues by Mohawk tribe
1644	Birth of William Penn; Christmas in England prohibited by Act of Parliament
1645	Death of St. John Masias on September 18 (John Masias was beatified by Pope Pius VII and canonized by Pope Paul VI in 1975.)
1648	End of the Thirty Years' War; founding of the Society of Friends (Quakers)

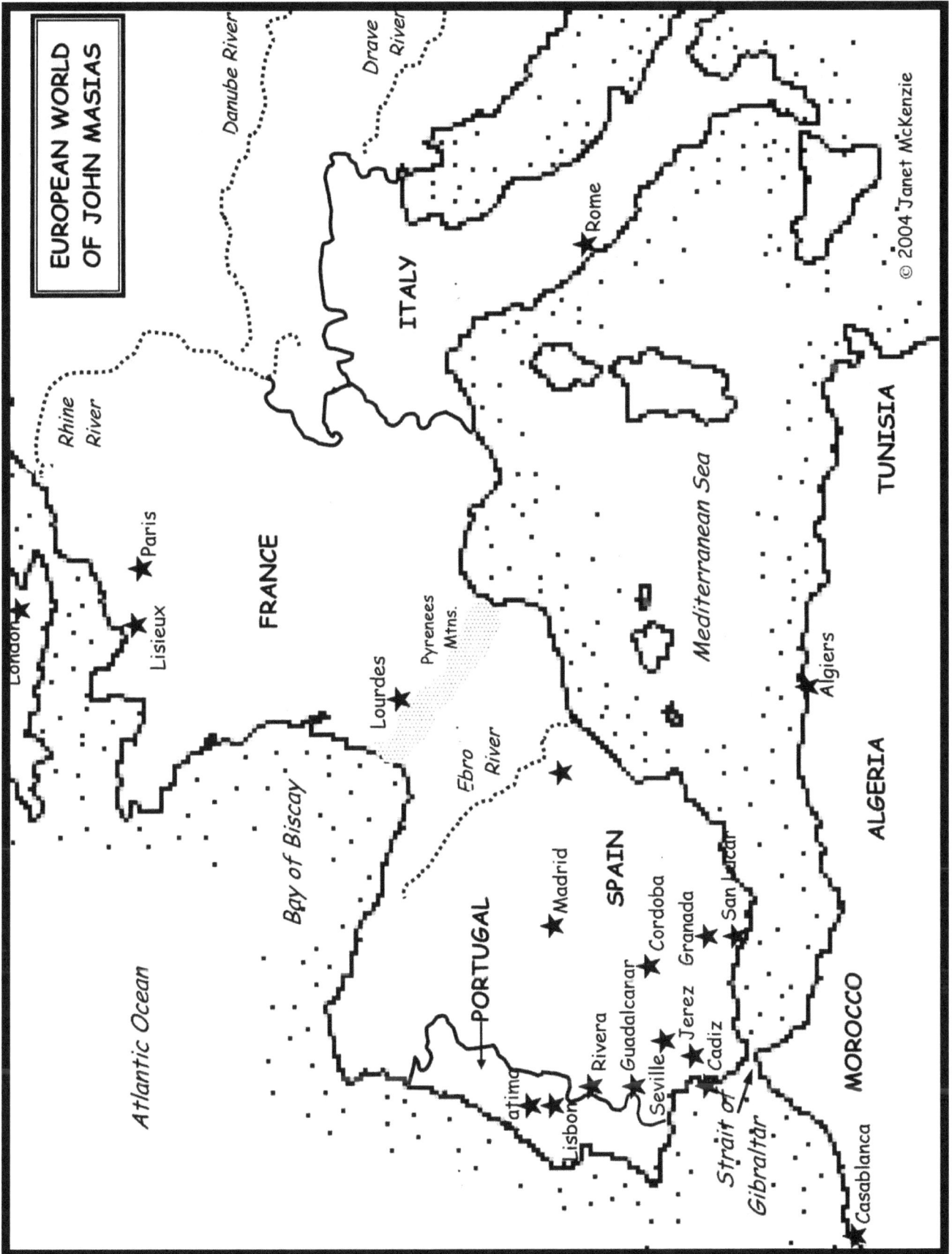

EUROPEAN WORLD
OF JOHN MASIAS

© 2004 Janet McKenzie

Danube River

Drave River

Rhine River

London

Paris

Lisieux

FRANCE

ITALY

Rome

Lourdes

Pyrenees Mtns.

Ebro River

Bay of Biscay

Atlantic Ocean

Mediterranean Sea

TUNISIA

Algiers

ALGERIA

Madrid

SPAIN

PORTUGAL

Cordoba

Guadalcanar

Granada

San Lucar

Rivera

Jerez

Seville

Cadiz

Fatima

Lisbon

Strait of Gibraltar

MOROCCO

Casablanca

HAITI

PUERTO RICO

Atlantic Ocean

Caribbean Sea

Barranquilla

Gulf of Darien

Cartagena

GUYANA

SURINAME

PANAMA

VENEZUELA

FRENCH GUIANA

Gulf of Gorgona

Bogota

COLUMBIA

EQUATOR

Quito

EQUATOR

EQUADOR

PERU

Callao
Lima

BRAZIL

BOLIVIA
Potosi

Pacific Ocean

Gran Chaco Plain

Tucumán

PARAGUAY

C
H
I
L
I

A
R
G
E
N
T
I
N
A

Córdoba

URUGUAY

Atlantic Ocean

SOUTH AMERICAN WORLD
OF ST. JOHN MASIAS'

Strait of Magellen

© Janet McKenzie 2004

Chapters 1 and 2–In Which John the Shepherd Becomes a Farmer

✴REVIEW✴ Vocabulary

on the edge of a little *embankment*   *patron*
Throughout the *ominous* mass   *Apostle(s)*

?? Comprehension Questions/Narration Prompts

1. What was St. John Masias' real name?
2. Why did John wish to go to America?
3. Who appeared to John in a vision? Where did the two of them go together?
4. What new job did John obtain in Guadalcanar?

Forming Opinions/Drawing Conclusions

1. Why do you think the traveler believed that praying the rosary for the Holy Souls in Purgatory is only for women? Do you agree? Why or why not?
2. Explain in your own words the relationship John had with his sister Mary.
3. Describe the miracle that occurred in Chapter 2. What might your reaction have been?

✝ Growing in Holiness

John prayed three rosaries every day—one each for the Holy Souls in Purgatory, for sinners, and for the growth of God's kingdom on earth. Although you may not always pray three rosaries a day, specify a particular intention for each decade of your rosary. Offer short prayers and small sacrifices throughout the day for specific intentions, especially for the Holy Souls in Purgatory who are unable to help themselves. (See page 60 of this study guide for additional prayers to the Holy Souls in Purgatory.)

Geography

Trace the map of Europe from page 51 of this guide. Label and color the four seas and oceans (and four rivers) blue. Label the Pyrenees Mountains, and color them brown.

📖 Searching Scripture

1. St. John the Evangelist greets John with "Peace be to you, little brother" (page 12). Read how Jesus greets His disciples in John 20:19 and 26.
2. St. John the Evangelist tells John that heaven is his true home (page 14). Read Hebrews 11:13-16 and Hebrews 13:14.
3. John saw a "gorgeous rainbow" (page 16). Read Genesis 9:12-17 and Sirach 43:11-12 (Ecclesiasticus 43:12-13).
4. "You have served God faithfully for twenty years, in the simple way He desired for you. Now you are to serve Him in great ways " (page 18). Read Matthew 25:21.

Chapters 3 and 4–In Which John at Last Goes to America

✦REVIEW✦ Vocabulary
not a man with whom anyone *trifled*   *Father Prior (Prior)*
left to his own *resources*   *Holy Faith*

⁇ Comprehension Questions/Narration Prompts
1. What was John's first and only job in Seville? How did it end?
2. Where did Father Peter suggest that John go?
3. Why was John better suited to become a lay brother instead of a friar (priest)?
4. How long did John stay at Jerez? What job did he have there? What was his relationship with the Dominican monastery there?

Forming Opinions/Drawing Conclusions
1. What did John see in the actions and suggestions of others that filled him with peace and led to his instant, cheerful obedience? How can you imitate this holy habit?
2. Why would it be difficult to be given a glimpse of heaven and then set back upon the earth to live? Consider what crosses heavenly gifts can sometimes bring.

✝ Growing in Holiness
St. John Masias gives us a good example of humility in action. Think of humility as not thinking less of yourself but thinking of yourself less. List several practical ways to change your attitude toward obedience in order to increase your humility. Ask your patron saint and guardian angel to help you.

Geography
Complete the map started in the previous lesson by labeling all cities red and the countries green. On the map provided, cities are indicated with a star; countries are in bold capitals. Draw an orange line showing John's travels from Rivera to Gaudalcanar to Seville to Jerez to San Lucar.

Timeline Work
Taping sheets of plain paper end-to-end, make a timeline representing the years from 1567 through 1648. Let three inches equal 25 years. Mark on your timeline the dates and events from 1567 through 1605, using information from page 50 of this study guide.

Searching Scripture
Consider ". . . the fine reward God has in store for those who serve Him faithfully" (page 31). Read 1 Corinthians 2:9-10.

Chapters 5 and 6—In Which John Joins the Dominican Order in Lima

❖REVIEW❖ Vocabulary

such a rigorous *regime*   *choir stall*
poor *raiment* of a beggar   *altar*

❓❓❓ Comprehension Questions/Narration Prompts

1. The travelers that John accompanied from Barranquilla to Bogota were happy to let John join them. Why?
2. Explain why Lima is called "The City of the Kings."
3. At what age did John decide to join the Dominican order? Why did he choose the monastery at St. Mary Magdalen?
4. What does Brother Paul claim is "one of the first rules in the religious life"?
5. What two remedies does John employ to send the devil fleeing?

💡 Forming Opinions/Drawing Conclusions

1. Why did John not stay and talk to the residents of San Lazaro?
2. What does the "spirit of abandonment" (page 54) mean?
3. In your own words, relate John's encounter with the devil.

📖 For Further Study

Research the earth's imaginary line, the Equator. What are the celestial and magnetic equators? Make a list of all the countries in the world that the equator goes through. (There are three in South America, six in Africa, and one in the western Pacific.)

✝ Growing in Holiness

John places great importance on the use of holy water against the devil. Obtain holy water from your church. Keep some available in holy water fonts around your home.

🗺 Geography

Trace the map of South America from page 52 of this study guide. Label and color the sea, gulfs, and oceans blue. Draw and color the Amazon River blue and the Andes Mountains brown. Label the countries (indicated in bold capitals) in green. Copy the dashed black line for the equator. Label the following cities in red: Cartagena, Barranquilla, Bogota, Quito, and Lima. Draw John's journey from Cartagena to Lima by way of Barranquilla.

✓ Checking the Catechism

Older students may read about the devil (the "Evil One" or "Satan") in the *Catechism of the Catholic Church* (*CCC*) text paragraphs 391-395 and 2850-2854 (74-75, 125, and 597).

Chapters 7 and 8—In Which John Adjusts to Religious Life and Grows in Wisdom

✖REVIEW✖ Vocabulary

the devil *plagued* him . . . constantly   *gatekeeper (porter)*
the required *dowry* be found   *chant*

???? Comprehension Questions/Narration Prompts

1. When did John Masias make his Dominican profession? How old was he?
2. For what purpose does Father Prior believe we are given friends?
3. What new job was John given a year or so after his Dominican profession?
4. What does John state are "the tools that will help any man to go to heaven"?

Forming Opinions/Drawing Conclusions

1. Explain John Masias' "secret of true peace" as outlined on pages 64 and 65.
2. In your own words, retell the story of the woman and the coat.
3. Relate some of the conversational topics of the two saints on their day off. What topics do you and your friends discuss on your free time?
4. Throughout this book, many references are made to America but in reference to South America. As residents of the United States of America, we often think of Americans only as people from our country. Expand your definition of Americans to include our fellow Americans from Canada, Mexico, and South America.

✝ Growing in Holiness

1. Father Prior states that one Hail Mary said devoutly will help someone go to heaven. He also talks about friendship. Each day devoutly pray one Hail Mary for a friend.
2. Saints are very much like ordinary people except they are more aware of God's presence in their lives. Twice in Chapter 7, John's prayers are immediately answered. Become more aware of God's presence in your life. Look for signs of God's answers to your prayers—even if it may not be the answers you seek.

Timeline Work

Add the dates and events from 1606 through 1624 to your timeline.

📖 Searching Scripture

1. ". . . never forget these two great commandments!" (page 73) Read Leviticus 19:18, Deuteronomy 6:4-9, Matthew 22:34-40, Romans 13:8-10, Galatians 5:14, and James 2:8.
2. ". . . become worthy images of God Himself" (page 79). Read Genesis 1:27 and Sirach (Ecclesiasticus) 17:1.

Chapters 9 and 10–In Which John Offers Prayers for and Advice to Others

---

⟨REVIEW⟩ Vocabulary

the *plight* of the unfortunate
with carefree *impudence*

venerated (*venerate*)
Church Militant

??? Comprehension Questions/Narration Prompts

1. What happened to the shopkeeper after he refused to give John alms?
2. What does John believe is the most important task in life?
3. Who appeared to John while he knelt before the Blessed Sacrament? What did they want from him?
4. What questions did John ask the boys in the orchard about their future?

Forming Opinions/Drawing Conclusions

1. ". . . brothers in Christ, no matter what their color, their education, their intelligence" (page 84). Search your conscience regarding your attitude toward others who may be different from you. Do you treat all people as brothers and sisters in Christ?
2. Other people living at the Magdalena tried to imitate John. "The result was a definite increase in virtue on the part of everyone" (page 93). What can you do to inspire virtue on the part of others you meet?
3. Retell the stories of the men who asked for John's advice and prayers in Chapter 10.

For Further Study

1. Research the office of gatekeeper (also referred to as porter). Once a minor order in the Church, this office was abolished in 1972. Read the description of the porter in Chapter 66 of The Rule of St. Benedict as found on page 60 of this study guide.
2. Research the life of Solanus Casey, a Capuchin porter born in Wisconsin in 1876, who was declared venerable by Pope John Paul II on July 11, 1995.

✝ Growing in Holiness

John knelt down in prayer for his new friends while they were present (page 102). At least once this week, pray for a friend in his/her presence.

Geography

Label the city of Callao in red on your map of South America.

✓ Checking the Catechism

Older students may read text paragraph 1330 (275) in the *CCC* ragarding the Blessed Sacrament. Younger students may review the Blessed Sacrament in their catechisms.

Chapters 11 and 12–In Which Many Miracles Are Attributed to John Masias

⭐REVIEW⭐ Vocabulary
resplendent in his royal robes   *chosen friend (soul)*
but to no *avail*   *Great Silence*

??? Comprehension Questions/Narration Prompts
1. Why did John kneel when he served food to the poor?
2. Other than serve them food, what else did John do for the poor?
3. What was special about the monastery donkey?
4. What was John's explanation for God sending suffering to people?
5. How long was John's general confession with Father Gonzalez?
6. How many souls did John Masias release from Purgatory with his prayers?

Forming Opinions/Drawing Conclusions
1. Compare John's prayer life (time before the tabernacle) and care of the poor with that of Mother Teresa of Calcutta's.
2. "Why can't Brother John act like the rest of us?" (page 109) Many people are uncomfortable around others who have holy habits or receive great gifts from God. Has anyone ever teased you about being "too holy"? How can you respond to this "accusation"?
3. Explain John's "door to joy."
4. Explain John's attitude toward God's answers to our prayers.
5. Summarize the miracles related in this story that were connected with John.
6. St. Teresa of Avila is quoted as saying, "One perfect soul can do more for God's glory than a thousand ordinary souls." How can you apply this saying to John Masias? What can you do to become more like a "perfect soul" and less like an ordinary one?

✝ Growing in Holiness
"It was his [John's] custom to spend two hours here every afternoon, telling his problems to Our Lord in the Blessed Sacrament" (page 108). Although you may not be able to spend two hours each day in prayer before the tabernacle, begin to spend at least ten minutes each day in prayer—either in front of the tabernacle or before a crucifix. Although you may also offer prayers of petition, spend at least five minutes offering praise and thanks to our dear Lord. Remember to pray in the name of Jesus Christ as John did.

📖 Searching Scripture
1. Regarding John's child-like trust (page 122), read Mark 10:15.
2. Read 1 Peter 2:21 regarding suffering.
3. John says he asks for blessings "in the Name of Jesus Christ" (page 132). Read John 14:13-14, John 16:23-24, and Ephesians 5:20.

Chapters 13 and 14—In Which John Goes to His Heavenly Home

✴REVIEW✴ Vocabulary

somber chant of the Requiem Mass   *prophecy*
much *abashed*   *Requiem Mass*

??? Comprehension Questions/Narration Prompts

1. Who was in John's room when Father Blaise came to see him shortly after John received Communion?
2. Name the five saints of Lima.
3. What did John Lopez do for John Masias shortly before John Masias died?
4. On what day did John die? How long was John at the Magdalena in Lima?
5. What was John's gift to Dona Antonia?

Forming Opinions/Drawing Conclusions

1. Retell the story of the fifteen plums.
2. Explain what the Prior meant when he said about John, "Only in the next world would the souls thus saved realize the goodness and charity of this hidden friend" (page 141).
3. What does the title of John Masias—"warrior in white" (page 146)—mean?

For Further Study

On the Internet, search for various churches that have been named in honor of St. John Masias. How many can you find? In how many countries are they located?

✝ Growing in Holiness

Make a list of holy habits you have learned from St. John Masias. Compose a short prayer to St. John, asking him to help you practice these habits regularly. Remember especially to invoke his help in overcoming sins against obedience and humility.

Geography

Label in red the city of Potosi to complete the map of South America.

Timeline Work

Complete your timeline by adding events from the years 1626 to 1648.

Searching Scripture

St. John Masias' last words were "Into Thy hands, O Lord, I commend my spirit!" (page 143). Read Luke 23:46.

The Rule of St. Benedict
Chapter 66 on the Porter of the Monastery

Let a wise old man be placed at the door of the monastery, one who knows how to take and give an answer, and whose mature age does not permit him to stray.

The porter should have a cell near the door that they who come may always find one present from whom they may obtain an answer. As soon as anyone knocks or a poor person calls, let him answer, "Thanks be to God," or invoke a blessing, and with the meekness of the fear of God let him return an answer speedily in the fervor of charity. If the porter has need of assistance, let him have a younger brother.

If it can be done, the monastery should be so situated that all the necessaries, such as water, the mill, the garden, are enclosed, and the various arts may be plied inside of the monastery, so that there may be no need for the monks to go about outside, because it is not good for their souls. But we desire that this Rule be read quite often in the community, that none of the brethren may excuse himself of ignorance.

Prayers for the Holy Souls in Purgatory

Prayer when passing a cemetery:
   "Eternal rest grant unto them, O Lord; and let perpetual light shine upon them. May they rest in peace. Amen."

Prayer to add to mealtime, morning and/or evening prayers or when offering a sacrifice:
   "Merciful Jesus, grant them everlasting rest. Amen."

The Seven Penitential Psalms can be recited for the souls detained in Purgatory:
   Psalm 6, Prayer in Time of Distress
   Psalm 32 (31), Remission of Sin
   Psalm 38 (37), Prayer of an Afflicted Sinner
   Psalm 51 (50), Prayer of Repentance (*Miserere*)
   Psalm 102 (101), Prayer in Time of Distress
   Psalm 130 (129), Prayer for Pardon and Mercy (*De Profundis*)
   Psalm 143 (142), Prayer of a Penitent in Distress

✎ Book Summary Test for *Saint John Masias*

Directions: Answer in complete sentences. If necessary, use the back page for additional writing space. (100 possible points, 20 points for each answer)

1. Who was John Masias' patron saint? In what ways did he help John?

   _____

   _____

2. Describe John's family life, his education, and the various jobs he had. In what country was John born? In what other country did he live?

   _____

   _____

   _____

3. To whom was St. John Masias particularly devoted?

   _____

   _____

4. How did St. John Masias save over one million souls?

   _____

   _____

5. What virtues and holy habits of St. John Masias' do you plan to incorporate into your own spiritual life?

   _____

   _____

   _____

   _____

   _____

   _____

Saint John Masias, *Marvelous Dominican Gatekeeper of Lima, Peru*

Answer Key to Comprehension Questions

Chapters 1 and 2—In Which John the Shepherd Becomes a Farmer

1. St. John Masias' real name was John d'Arcos. He took his uncle's name of Masias as John's father died when John was about five years old.
2. John wanted to go to America not to obtain a fortune in gold or silver—the reason most people of his time wanted to go—but because he felt it was God's Will for him to be of use to the poor and ignorant there.
3. John's patron saint, St. John the Evangelist, appeared to John in a vision. Together the two of them traveled in spirit to heaven, and then to Guadalcanar. (Note the typographical error on page 12 of the Tan edition of this biography, "One bright summer morning in the year 1665." This should read "in the year 1605.")
4. In Guadalcanar, John obtained a job with a farmer, tending crops and cattle.

Chapters 3 and 4—In Which John at Last Goes to America

1. John's first and only job in Seville lasted for only several hours. He was put in charge of a sidewalk pastry stand for an hour, an hour that stretched into several hours. He was robbed of all the stand's goods and money by the owner's sons. When the owner returned, John was beaten; and his own possessions were stolen. John was rescued by Father Peter of the Dominican church in Seville.
2. Father Peter suggested (and in this suggestion, John saw the will of God) that John go to the Dominican friary in Jerez de la Frontera to pursue a religious vocation.
3. John was better suited to become a lay brother instead of a friar as John had had very little education and was therefore not prepared for the study required of a friar (priest).
4. John stayed at Jerez for fourteen years. While there, he did odd jobs around the Dominican monastery as well as about the town. He maintained close contact with the Dominican friary but did not pursue admission there as either a friar or a lay brother.

Chapters 5 and 6—In Which John Joins the Dominican Order in Lima

1. The travelers that John accompanied from Barranquilla to Bogota were happy to have him with them because through his prayers they had been protected from attacks by the native tribes, they had never run out of food, and they had not been stricken with the fever that was common in the region.
2. Lima is called "The City of the Kings" as it was founded on the Feast of the Epiphany, the day that the Church celebrates the Wise Men's visitation with the Infant Jesus.
3. John was thirty-seven years old when he decided to join the Dominican order. He chose the monastery at St. Mary Magdalen as it had a stricter regime, and he felt called to a life of prayer and penance.
4. Brother Paul claims that obedience is "one of the first rules in the religious life" (page 54).
5. In order to send the devil fleeing, John makes use of holy water as well as the holy names of Jesus, Mary, and Joseph.

Chapters 7 and 8—In Which John Adjusts to Religious Life and Grows in Wisdom

1. John Masias made his Dominican profession (the initial vows taken upon entrance to a religious community) on January 25, 1623, when he was thirty-seven years old.
2. Father Prior stated that we are given friends to help us save our souls—to lead us to God.
3. Slightly more than one year after his profession into the Dominican order, John was given the job of gatekeeper (porter) for the Dominican monastery of St. Mary Magdalen in Lima.
4. John states that "the tools that will help any man to go to heaven" are the two great commandments of Jesus: "love of God, then love of neighbor" (page 73).

Chapters 9 and 10—In Which John Offers Prayers and Advice to Others

1. After he refused to give alms to John Masias, the shopkeeper, Don Francisco, did not have a single customer purchase goods in his store until he went to John and apologized.
2. John believed that the most important task we have in life is to save our souls.
3. While he knelt before the Blessed Sacrament, hundreds of suffering souls from Purgatory appeared before John begging for his prayers.
4. John simply asked the boys in the orchard how old they would be in one hundred and two hundred years. In this way, he was able to get them to understand that while their bodies would be buried by then, their souls would still be alive. He got them to question whether or not they were making any effort to ensure that their souls would be worthy of heaven.

Chapters 11 and 12— In Which Many Miracles Are Attributed to John Masias

1. John knelt when he served food to the poor as he saw Christ in all the needy men and women. "I feel as though I were before the Tabernacle." (page 106)
2. Other than serve them food—which fed their physical bodies—he also taught them the truths contained in the catechism to feed their spiritual hunger.
3. The monastery donkey, trained by John under the guidance of St. John the Evangelist, went out begging for food from house to house by himself.
4. John believed that God sent suffering to people "because that is the only way to make certain people turn to Him" (page 123).
5. John's general confession with Father Gonzalez, which John made shortly before his death, lasted for three days. During this time, John was frequently interrupted by Father Gonzalez to obtain information about his youth as requested by the Prior for the monastery's records.
6. John was told by his patron saint St. John the Evangelist that through his prayers and sacrifices more than one million souls had been released from Purgatory.

Chapters 13 and 14—In Which John Goes to His Heavenly Home

1. When Father Blaise came to see John shortly after John received Communion, John told Father Blaise that the room was full of visitors—our Lord, the Blessed Mother, and many saints—who were waiting to take him to heaven.
2. The five saints of Lima are St. Turibius Alphonsus de Mogrovejo, St. Rose of Lima, St. Martin de Porres, St. Francis Solano, and St. John Masias.
3. Shortly before John Masias died, he sent John Lopez to Spain to deliver some money and a personal greeting to his sister Mary.
4. St. John Masias died on September 18, 1645. He had served at the Dominican monastery of St. Mary Magdalen in Lima for twenty-three years as a lay brother.
5. John's parting gift to Dona Antonia was the spiritual gift of courage and resignation to the Holy Will of God.

Answer Key to Book Summary Test

1. John Masias' patron saint was St. John the Evangelist. St. John the Evangelist appeared to St. John Masias several times with messages from God. He also helped St. John Masias travel around Spain. Later, he helped St. John Masias to train the monastery donkey to beg for food to donate to the poor.
2. John and his sister Mary were orphaned when John was five years old and his sister was two. They lived for a while with John's uncle and adopted his name. For most of his young life, John lived with a farmer, tending his sheep. He received very little formal education. When John was around twenty years old, he went to Guadalcanar, Spain, and worked for a farmer for several weeks. He then moved to Jerez and worked various odd jobs around the town and Dominican monastery. Fourteen years later, the Father Prior of the monastery recommended John for an accounting job on board a ship headed for South America. John then worked in Lima, Peru, for two and one-half years on a ranch before entering the Do-

minican monastery of St. Mary Magdalen at the age of thirty-seven. St. John Masias worked as the gatekeeper of this monastery until his death twenty-three years later.

3. St. John Masias had a special devotion to his patron saint, St. John the Evangelist. He also had a great devotion to the Holy Souls in Purgatory, the Blessed Mother, and Jesus in the tabernacle. He devoted much of his life serving the poor in whom he saw Christ Himself.

4. St. John the Evangelist told St. John Masias that through his prayers and sacrifices he had freed over one million souls from Purgatory.

5. Answers will vary.

Study Guide for

Saint Benedict, The Story of the Father of the Western Monks

St. Benedict

St. Benedict lived in the early Mid Ages.
He wrote a great Rule that took many pages.
He started out small,
And then did install
Monks from the unlearned and wisest of sages.

He started in Rome, then moved to a cave,
Fasting and praying for how we behave.
They asked him to lead.
It didn't succeed.
So Benedict left, returned to his cave.

Men flocked to him. He grew crops from some seed.
Children too joined him; he taught them to read.
Wonders occurred there
With help of his prayer.
The devil despised him—tried to mislead.

So Benedict left there to start over again.
He chose Monte Cassino and there did begin.
An order to found
One that would abound
In work, prayer and peace, its victory to win.

He became a great abbot and welcomed the poor—
Didn't think they should be turned away from his door.
To leaders he talked,
To his place they walked.
His influence with them we can not ignore.

His order endured after he died;
The Rule that he left served as their guide.
It continues today;
Benedictines obey
Almost unchanged the Rule he supplied.

Think what you can learn from this saint and his tale.
How you can apply it to help you prevail.
Then mold what you do
And boldly pursue
His pattern of holiness. Follow his trail.

Timeline of Events

Year	Event
329	Birth of St. Basil the Great (died 379)
340	Birth of St. Ambrose, Bishop of Milan (died in 397)
406	St. Jerome completed the Latin Vulgate of the Bible
408-450	Theodosius II ruled Eastern Roman empire
410	Alaric, King of the Visigoths, sacked Rome
411	St. Augustine (354-430) wrote *The City of God*
432	St. Patrick consecrated Bishop of Ireland
440-461	Leo the Great reigned as Pope
453	Death of Attila the Hun
455	Vandals sacked Rome under King Genseric (395-477)
476	Roman Empire fell under leadership of Odoacer (434-493)
480	Birth of Benedict
493	Birth of Theodoric, King of the Ostrogoths (died in 526)
496	Conversion of Clovis, King of the Franks
497	Benedict left his Roman school to become a hermit
500	Benedict established monks at Subiaco; construction of the Vatican Palace began
522	Benedict accepted Placid and Maurus as Oblates
527	Benedict founded the Order of St. Benedict at Monte Cassino
527-565	Justinian ruled as emperor of the Byzantine empire; rebuilding of the Church of the Nativity, Bethlehem
528	Benedict completes his Rule
529	Justinian's Code of Civil Laws issued
532-537	Construction of St. Sophie Cathedral
535	Justinian invades Italy
536	Placid established a Benedictine monastery in Sicily (died 540)
537	Death of King Arthur, legendary figure
540	Totila of Italy (King of Ostrogoths until 552)
542	Benedict meets with King Totila; Plague in Europe
543	Earthquakes throughout Europe
547	Death of Benedict's twin sister, St. Scholastica on February 10th; death of St. Benedict on March 21st
553	Second Council of Constantinople
570	Birth of Mohammed, founder of Islam (died 632)
581	Monte Cassino destroyed by the Lombards
590	Gregory the Great elected Pope (540-604)
596	St. Augustine of Canterbury began evangelization of England

AGE OF MIGRATIONS
Late 4th to Early 6th Centuries

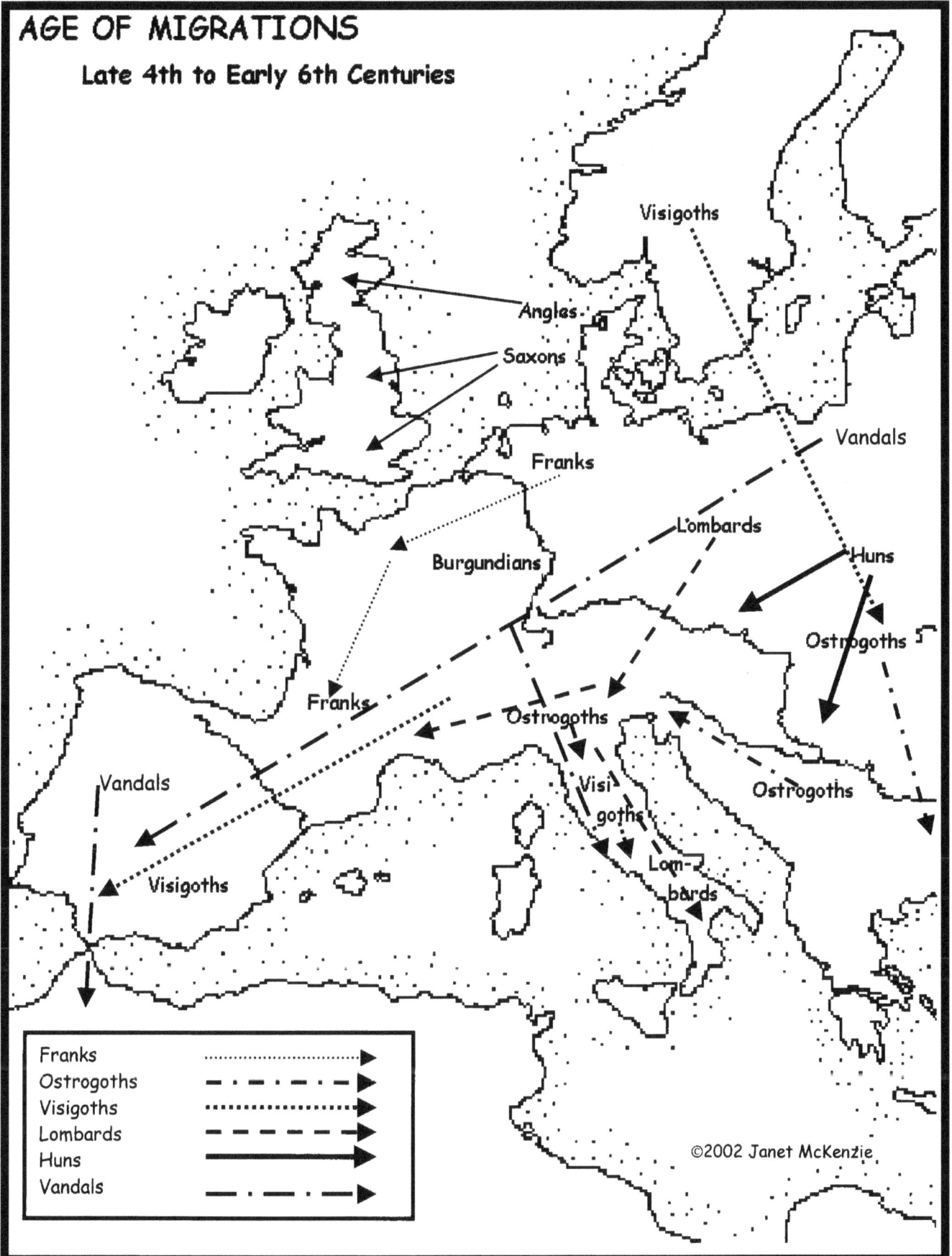

Visigoths

Angles

Saxons

Franks

Vandals

Lombards

Burgundians

Huns

Franks

Ostrogoths

Vandals

Ostrogoths

Visigoths

Ostrogoths

Visi goths

Lom-bards

Visigoths

Franks	·············▶
Ostrogoths	—·—·—·▶
Visigoths	··········▶
Lombards	— — — ▶
Huns	━━━━▶
Vandals	—··—··—▶

©2002 Janet McKenzie

ROMAN ROADS IN ITALY AROUND 500 AD
"All roads lead to Rome"

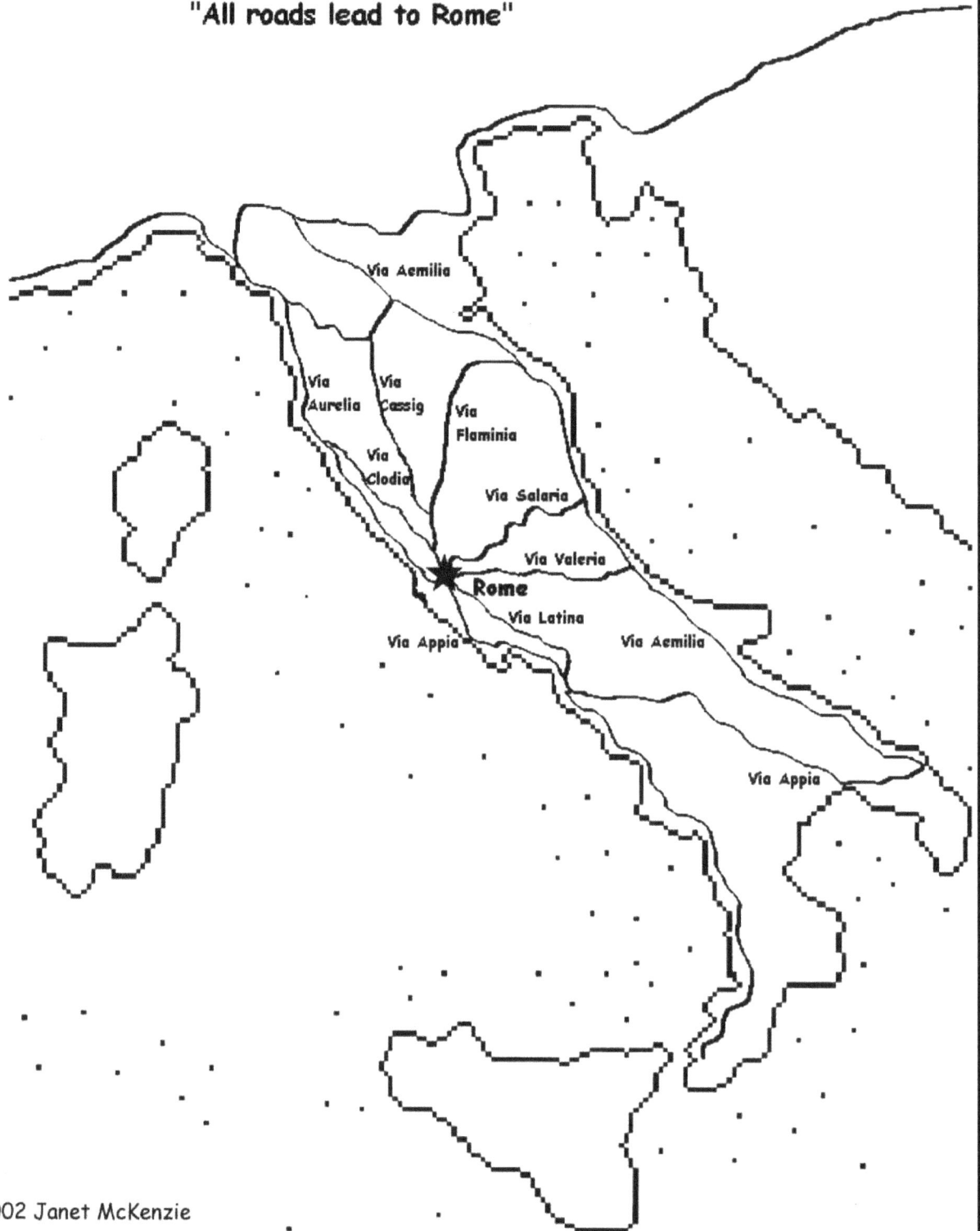

Via Aemilia

Via Aurelia

Via Cassig

Via Clodia

Via Flaminia

Via Salaria

Via Valeria

Rome

Via Latina

Via Appia

Via Aemilia

Via Appia

©2002 Janet McKenzie

Chapters 1 and 2–In Which Benedict Decides to Become a Hermit and Performs His First Miracle

---

✶REVIEW✶ Vocabulary

a leader in law or *politics*   *hermit*
the *spire* of a little church   *vocation*

⁇⁇ Comprehension Questions/Narration Prompts

5. Why did Benedict leave Rome? Where was he headed?
6. What did Benedict feel all the saints possessed "in abundance"?
7. Why did Benedict leave Enfide?

💡 Forming Opinions/Drawing Conclusions

List at least three positive and three negative aspects of a hermit's life.

📖 For Further Study

Benedict relates how he spotted the spire of a church before entering Enfide. Research architecture from this time period, especially St. Sophia Cathedral. St. Sophia, whom some say is the finest example of Byzantine architecture in the world, was built by Justinian between 532 and 537 (during Benedict's lifetime) in Constantinople, which is now Istanbul. (Note: St. Sophia Cathedral was not named after a saint but is translated as "holy wisdom.")

Discover the difference between a *spire*, a *steeple*, and a *turret*. How many sides does a spire usually have?

✝ Growing in Holiness

Benedict stated: "I want to spend my life praying for people who don't bother to pray for themselves" (page 9). Begin today to pray one Our Father and one Hail Mary for all sinners, especially those who will die today.

📅 Timeline Work

Taping sheets of plain paper end-to-end, make a timeline representing the years from 325 through 600. Let three inches equal 25 years. Mark on your timeline the dates and events from 329 through 480, using information from page 68 of this study guide.

📖 Searching Scripture

Benedict wished to increase his faith. Read Luke 17:5-6 for Jesus' response.

Chapters 3 and 4–Which Relate How Benedict Lived as a Hermit and How His Life as an Abbot at Vicovaro Was Brief

✗REVIEW✗ Vocabulary
a rough *tunic* made of sheepskins   *monk*
unlettered peasants   *consecrated*

??? Comprehension Questions/Narration Prompts
1. What two virtues belong to all great souls and were not lacking in Benedict?
2. What did the monks of Vicovaro feel was a major qualification for an abbot?
3. What two virtues did Benedict feel were most important in the monastic life?

Forming Opinions/Drawing Conclusions
1. Expand on Benedict's statement that "man's chief task in this world is to seek God and praise His goodness" (page 17).
2. Remembering that Benedict was seventeen when he left Rome, state how long he remained a hermit at Subiaco.
3. Benedict discusses how men in the world "clutch eagerly at the hours" (page 21). Note how Benedict uses his time compared to men attached to the world.

For Further Study
Benedict has been given the title of the "Father of Western Monasticism." Study the role of Benedictine monks in history. Aside from their spiritual contributions, research the various roles they played in the Middle Ages: providing medical care and other assistance to the local community; advancing the science of agriculture; opening schools and other centers of learning; fostering Gregorian chant; working as artists, scholars, vintners, and doctors; and perhaps most importantly, preserving in their *scriptoria* many works of the Greeks and Romans as well as handwritten copies of Scripture, many with beautiful illuminations. Research the online Catholic Encyclopedia at www.newadvent.org/cathen.

Growing in Holiness
"Why should he seek for comforts when presented with a good chance to suffer for his own sins and those of men and women living in the world" (page 20)? Find at least three opportunities this week to choose sacrifice over comfort. Offer your sacrifices for someone you know who is in need of spiritual assistance.

Searching Scripture
Benedict exhorts us to "keep on with our prayers and good works" (page 19). Read James 2:14-26.

Chapters 5 and 6–In Which Placid and Maurus Join the Monks at Subiaco, and Benedict Prays for the Three Monasteries atop the Mountain

---

✸REVIEW✸ Vocabulary

the *peasants* at Subiaco   *desert hermits*
a dark and forbidding *chasm*   *Oblate*

??? Comprehension Questions/Narration Prompts

1. How many men joined Benedict in his original colony at Subiaco?
2. What was Benedict's motto in Latin? What is the English translation?
3. According to Benedict, what must one do to have lasting happiness?

Forming Opinions/Drawing Conclusions

Relate how the lives of the peasants/monks were changed after joining Benedict. Include information such as the political state of the surrounding countryside, the difference in the monks' lives, and their reasons for joining—and staying with—Benedict. (Gather information from pages 30, 31, and 38.)

For Further Study

Research the various leaders mentioned in Chapter 5 and the tribes they led: Theodoric (Ostrogoths), Alaric (Visigoths), Attila (Huns), and Genseric (Vandals). Find out when each leader lived, where they came from, where they eventually settled, and who, in turn, may have defeated them. Refer the map entitled "The Age of Migrations" on page 69 of this guide. Summarize your research in a brief report, outline, or oral presentation.

✝ Growing in Holiness

Benedict goes off at night to pray for his needs just as Jesus often did. Jesus states that we are not to stand on the street corner and pray but rather pray in our rooms in secret (Matthew 6:5-6). This week spend some time each day quietly praying in your room in imitation of Jesus and St. Benedict.

Timeline Work

Add the dates and events between 493 and 522 to your timeline.

✓ Checking the Catechism

Older students may read text paragraphs 2623-43 (550-556) in the *Catechism of the Catholic Church* (*CCC*) on the five forms of prayer. Younger students may research references to prayer, forms of prayer, and methods of praying in their own catechisms. If desired, complete Activity #64 in *100 Activities Based on the Catechism of the Catholic Church*.

Chapters 7 and 8–In Which Three Miracles Occur, and Florentius Causes Benedict to Leave Subiaco

---

✖REVIEW✖ Vocabulary

Father Abbot's *cowl* over my head   *toil, nobility of*
consternation among the monks   *eulogia*

??? Comprehension Questions/Narration Prompts

1. Name the three miracles that occur in Chapter 7.
2. What did Benedict decide to do in response to the unkindness of Florentius?
3. Why did Benedict leave Subiaco? Who became abbot in his place?

Forming Opinions/Drawing Conclusions

1. Discuss "an obedience prompt and humble" (page 45). What behaviors or attitudes do you need to change in order to make your obedience "prompt and humble"?
2. Which of the three miracles of Chapter 7 do you consider the greatest? Explain.
3. "He preaches the nobility of toil" (page 53). Discuss the value of all work. Is its value different today than it was in the sixth century?

For Further Study

Research the Arian heresy, which began in the fourth century. This heresy denied the divinity of Christ, the eternal nature of God, and Jesus as the Son of God. In 325 the Council of Nicea was convened to combat this heresy and wrote a creed to support the truths of the faith. This heresy was one of the most far-reaching heresies of the Church. Research Arius (256-326) and St. Athanasius (296-373). Memorize the Nicene Creed.

✝ Growing in Holiness

"Turn away from evil and do good. Seek after peace and pursue it" (page 59). Memorize this passage. Then put it into practice; try always to be a peacemaker. (Note: Benedict's motto is taken from Psalm 34 (33):15 if you wish to check. Perhaps there is a different verse from Psalms that you would like to adopt as your own personal motto.)

Searching Scripture

1. Read what Scripture teaches about the value of labor: Psalm 90 (89):17, Proverbs 14:23, Ecclesiastes 9:10, Ephesians 4:28, and Titus 3:14.
2. Pages 50-51 and pages 54-55 contain several references to scriptural passages. Match the following Biblical passages with the appropriate passages in these two chapters: Mark 6:45-51, Matthew 19:26, Matthew 5:43-48, Matthew 6:9-15, and Luke 18:14.

Chapters 9 and 10–In Which Benedict Establishes the Monastery at Monte Cassino, and the Devil Causes Trouble

✦REVIEW✦ Vocabulary

to offer *homage* to Jupiter   *merits*
The *obstinate* rock   *habit*

??? Comprehension Questions/Narration Prompts

1. What did Benedict do in order to better discern God's plan for himself as well as his monks? What was the result?
2. Why was the devil upset about Benedict's decision to build a monastery at Monte Cassino? What did the devil do to upset Benedict's plan?
3. What miracle occurred in Chapter 10 as a result of Benedict's intercession?

Forming Opinions/Drawing Conclusions

1. ". . . no one who understood the truths of the Christian Faith" (page 62). List several truths all Christians share. Name some truths that are embraced only by Catholics.
2. Explain this description of the devil: "the father of jealousy and pride" (page 66).

For Further Study

Research these Roman gods and goddess and discover what influence they had on Roman culture and history: Apollo, god of the sun; Jupiter, ruler of gods and men; and Venus, goddess of love and beauty.

✝ Growing in Holiness

Benedict's monks relate that the devil tried to get Benedict's attention by calling his name; when this was unsuccessful, he tried other methods. St. Benedict is a powerful intercessor against the devil. The St. Benedict medal is one of the oldest and most highly honored medals of the Church. Because of the number of miracles attributed to it, it has become known as the "devil-chasing medal." These medals can be attached to a scapular or worn about the neck on a chain. They are readily available from Catholic retailers.

The front of the medal has St. Benedict standing before an altar holding a cross with the words in Latin, which translate as, "Cross of our Father Benedict" and "May we be protected in our death by His presence." The back has the cross of St. Benedict and numerous letters which stand for the following: "Get thee behind me, Satan," "Persuade me not to vanity," "The cup you offer is evil," "Drink the poison yourself," "May the sacred cross be my light," "Let not the devil be my guide." The older versions of the medal also have "That in all things God be glorified."

Memorize several of these ejaculations. Recite them when you are tempted to sin. Call on St. Benedict to come to your aid in times of temptation.

Chapters 11 and 12–In Which Benedict Writes His Rule and Teaches His Monks the Peace That Comes from Humility and Obedience

REVIEW Vocabulary

guarded by ninety-two *galleys*   *Rule of St. Benedict*
the Emperor's victorious *legions*   *chanting of the Psalms*

??? Comprehension Questions/Narration Prompts

1. Why did Benedict disapprove of Justinian's decision to wage war in Italy?
2. What topics of monastic life did Benedict's Rule cover?

Forming Opinions/Drawing Conclusions

1. Discuss the possible pitfalls of life as a hermit as outlined on pages 76 and 77. Relate this to Benedict's writing of his Rule.
2. Expand on Benedict's link between obedience and humility as explained on page 78.
3. Connect the title of Chapter 11, "The Way of Peace," with the story told in Chapter 12.

For Further Study

Research the reign of Justinian, who reigned from 532 to 565 AD—the most glorious reign in Byzantine history. He built the great cathedral of St. Sophia; attemptted to reestablish the old Roman Empire in southern Spain, Africa, and Italy; and codified the laws that were based on the old Roman laws. This codex or *corpus juris*—body of law—filled three volumes and took him from 529 until the end of his reign to complete. This code of law influenced the laws of nearly all the European countries. Compare and contrast what laws would be included in Justinian's Code with the contents of the Rule of Benedict.

Growing in Holiness

Remember Benedict's connection between humility and obedience, and pride and disobedience. The next time you are tempted to disobey, or complain about obedience, or are sluggish in performing your obedience, say a prayer to your guardian angel or St. Benedict to help you overcome your pride and to submit to obedience. Observe this behavior in others and pray silently for them when you see them struggle with these virtues too.

Timeline Work

Add the dates and events from 527 through 535 to your timeline.

Searching Scripture

Read about peace in Psalm 119 (118):165, Proverbs 12:20, Baruch 3:13, Matthew 5:9, John 16:33, Romans 12:18 & 14:19, Philippians 4:9, and Hebrews 12:14.

Chapters 13 and 14–In Which Benedict's Monks Establish More Monasteries, and Benedict Teaches the Value of Obedience

---

✦REVIEW✦ Vocabulary

the well-traveled *Latin Way*   *bishop*
a handsome *villa* near the town   *sub-deacon*

??? Comprehension Questions/Narration Prompts

1. What three valuable gifts that Benedict received are mentioned in Chapter 13?
2. What is Benedict's advice to the monks establishing the monastery in Terracina?
3. What three promises had Brother Michael made when he entered Monte Cassino?
4. What two valuable lessons did Brother Michael learn in the story in Chapter 14?

Forming Opinions/Drawing Conclusions

1. Explain what the title to Chapter 13, "Distant Harvest" means.
2. Tell where Benedict's three new monasteries were to be located. Why did he choose those locations?

For Further Study

Research the Roman method of road construction. Write a step-by-step description of how these roads were built. Include the materials used and thickness of each layer and the width of the road. Use and define such words as *crown* (How high should it ideally be?), *scoop ditch*, *boundary ditch*, *road surface*, *agger*, and *metalling*. Draw a road cross-section to accompany your presentation. If desired, build a model of a Roman road.

Geography

Trace and label the map of Italy from page 70 of this guide. Trace over the Roman roads in red. Color the four seas and rivers blue. Color the two mountain ranges brown. Add the cities of Naples and Sicily. With the help of an atlas, label the three islands.

✝ Growing in Holiness

The Rule of Benedict emphasizes that all guests be received as though they were Christ Himself and no one in need must ever be turned away. Put this into practice by graciously welcoming all who come to your door. You may be like Abraham in Genesis 18:1-10 and entertain the Lord unawares! Perhaps you may entertain angels (Hebrews 13:2.).

Searching Scripture

Benedict miraculously filled an empty barrel. Read of similar miracles in Scripture: 1 Kings (3 Kings) 17:7-16 and John 2:1-10.

Chapters 15 and 16–In Which Benedict Shows the Power of Faith, Hope, and Charity

REVIEW Vocabulary
remained *aloof* from war   *pilgrim*
who delighted in *plaguing* Catholics   *shrine*

??? Comprehension Questions/Narration Prompts
1. List at least three miracles related in Chapter 15 that are attributed to Benedict.
2. What was another name for the monastery on Monte Cassino?
3. According the Brother Joseph, how can we conquer our weariness in the long struggle for perfection? What is opportunity that awaits us when we feel most downhearted?

Forming Opinions/Drawing Conclusions
Read the excerpt from the Rule of St. Benedict that Ms. Windeatt gives on page 114. List several family customs, behaviors, attitudes and habits that would be changed if this rule were applied to your life. How difficult would it be to not own any possessions?

For Further Study
There is no better way to learn of the spirituality of St. Benedict than to read his Rule. The Rule of St. Benedict is a complete set of guidelines written by St. Benedict to establish his monks within a self-supporting and community-minded monastery. Encouraging moderation as the ideal, it regulated almost every aspect of the monastic life. In its entirety, the Rule consists of about thirty pages the size of this study guide. The monks of Benedict were expected to memorize the entire Rule and be able to recite specific passages upon request. Research the role Benedict's rule had in monasteries for centuries after his death; his Rule is still used virtually unchanged by Benedictine monasteries for men as well as women today. The Rule is available on the Internet at various sites including www.christdesert.org (then select "St. Benedict" and then "Study the Holy Rule" on the left).

Growing in Holiness
Zalla converted to Christianity and gave up his persecution of Catholics because of the prayers and actions of Benedict. Today many souls go to hell, as they have no one to pray for them. Resolve to recite the Fatima Pardon Prayer seven times per day—the number of times the monks prayed per day—for at least a week for the conversion of sinners. "My God, I believe, I adore, I trust, and I love You. I beg pardon of You for those who do not believe, do not adore, do not trust, and do not love You."

Do not allow the Devil to convince you that these daily prayers are unimportant or unnecessary. "The Devil is always trying to make us break our good resolutions" (page 117). If you become weak in your resolve, make the Sign of the Cross for strength and in recognition of the power of God as the peasant did at the end of Chapter 15.

Chapters 17 and 18–In Which Benedict Proves Himself a Prophet to King Totila and Tells Maurus the Story of King Clovis

---

✖REVIEW✖ Vocabulary
bubonic plague was creeping
angry men paying him *deference*

cloister
prophet

??? Comprehension Questions/Narration Prompts
1. Describe what happened to Placid.
2. What four things did Benedict beg of God as he regarded the worldliness of man?
3. What prophesy did Benedict give to King Totila?
4. What prophesies were contained in the letter Benedict gave to Maurus upon Maurus' departure from Monte Cassino?

Forming Opinions/Drawing Conclusions
1. Explain this quotation of Benedict's from page 127, "The sword of sorrow is a deadly weapon . . . the fruit is bitter for all concerned."
2. If all people in the world knew that they only had ten years left to live, what changes do you see happening to people? What changes do you foresee happening in the world?

For Further Study
Research the life of Clovis, a king of the Franks in Gaul (France) from 481 to 511, who married a Catholic Burgundian princess named Clotildis and converted to the Christian faith.

✝ Growing in Holiness
In a time of war and violence, Benedict preached peace. Humility, obedience, and peace are the dominant themes of his Rule. Reflect on, memorize, and recite often the Path to Holiness prayer of Mother Teresa of Calcutta: "The fruit of silence is prayer; the fruit of prayer is faith; the fruit of faith is love; the fruit of love is service; and the fruit of service is peace."

Timeline Work
Add the dates and events from 536 through 542 to your timeline.

Searching Scripture
Benedict displays his gift of prophecy. Read about the various gifts God gives His followers in Ephesians 4:11-13 and 1 Corinthians 12:4-11. What other gifts mentioned in these passages did Benedict possess?

Chapters 19 and 20–In Which Benedict Reflects on the Path to Heaven and Sees into the Future

---

⟪REVIEW⟫ Vocabulary

the *seclusion* of this upper room   *catacombs*
worn out by *tempest*   *Paradise*

??? Comprehension Questions/Narration Prompts

1. What was Benedict's vision the night Bishop Germanus of Capua died?
2. What did the Benedictine monks believe about manual labor?
3. What was the vision Benedict received that cause him to convulse with great sobs?

💡 Forming Opinions/Drawing Conclusions

Benedict's motto—"Turn away from evil and do good. Seek peace and pursue it" (page 141)—expresses his vision for a heaven on earth. Discuss what would have to change—for individuals, for communities, for rulers of nations—for this vision to become reality. What can one person do to further this vision of peace?

📖 For Further Study

Benedict had a vision in which barbarians destroyed his monastery. Since the time of St. Benedict, Monte Cassino has been destroyed five times, the last time being in 1943 during World War II. The Lombards destroyed the monastery of Monte Cassino for the first time in 581. Research the Lombards, a German tribe whose name means "longbeard." (See also the "The Age of Migrations" map on page 69 of this guide.)

✝ Growing in Holiness

The Oblates and monks began memorization of the Psalms as soon as they arrived at Monte Cassino (page 140). Remember that all books in St. Benedict's time were handwritten; a copy of the Bible was a rare treasure. In order to pray the Psalms, they had to be recited from memory. To understand the extent of this memorization, remember that they were expected to memorize the Rule—about 30 typewritten pages, and the 150 Psalms—about sixty-five typewritten pages.

Review the book of Psalms. Select one Psalm of praise and memorize it. Use it often to offer praise to God—maybe seven times a day in imitation of the Benedictine monks.

✓ Checking the Catechism

How does the Our Father relate to Benedict's vision of peace? Older students read text paragraphs 2761-66, 2803-06, and 2857-2865 on the Our Father. Younger students may study references to the Our Father in their own catechisms. If desired, complete Activity #2 in *100 Activities*.

Chapters 21 and 22–In Which Benedict Meets with Scholastica for the Last Time and Goes to His Eternal Reward

---

✴REVIEW✴ Vocabulary

partake of the simple meal   *rule*
as his strength *ebbed*   *dispense*

??? Comprehension Questions/Narration Prompts

1. What did Benedict and his twin sister Scholastica have in common?
2. Summarize the events in Italy that occurred in Benedict's lifetime, 480 to 547.
3. What did Scholastica ask of God as the time for her annual meeting with Benedict came near an end?
4. Where did Benedict wish to be buried?

💡 Forming Opinions/Drawing Conclusions

1. Benedict spent the night with his sister describing the "beauties of Heaven" (page 149). Share your vision of what heaven is like, describing its delight for all the senses.
2. When near death, Benedict prays that his life has been pleasing to God. Describe four achievements of Benedict's that gave God glory and promoted His kingdom.

📖 For Further Study

Research the life of St. Gregory the Great (540-604). Gregory lived for several years as a Benedictine monk before being elected pope, an office he held for only fourteen years. He did much to establish unity and order during a difficult time. While he did not invent the chant, he is responsible for gathering the chants into one book and ensuring their proper use during the liturgy. He also sent missionaries to England and helped weave much of the Roman and Greek culture into the new civilization.

✝ Growing in Holiness

Benedict and Scholastica looked forward to their yearly meetings, which consisted of hours and hours of spiritual discussion. In imitation of these great saints, share the following biblical passages with a friend, parent, or sibling: Psalm 84 (83):2-13; John 14:1-3; Acts 7:55-56; 1 Corinthians 2:9-10. Recruit a friend or family member as your spiritual companion. If you can think of no one to fill this role, keep it in prayer. In the meantime, follow the advice of St. Scholastica: "I asked you to hear me and you would not. I asked the Lord and He heard me" (page 148). God is always there with open arms and ears.

📅 Timeline Work

Add the dates and events from 543 through 596 to complete your timeline.

✎ Book Summary Test for *Saint Benedict*

Directions: Answer in complete sentences. If necessary, use the back of the page for additional writing space. 100 possible points, 20 points for each answer.

1. What made St. Benedict decide to leave his studies in Rome and become a hermit?

    _____

    _____

2. What made him decide to leave his life as a hermit?

    _____

    _____

3. What were St. Benedict's mottoes? Explain each. (This book mentions three mottoes.)

    _____

    _____

    _____

    _____

4. What are the prominent themes of St. Benedict's Rule? Which of these did he con-sider as a "ladder to heaven"?

    _____

    _____

    _____

5. Describe in as much detail as you can, the social, religious and political climate in which St. Benedict lived. Name other key persons who lived at the same time.

    _____

    _____

    _____

    _____

    _____

Saint Benedict, The Story of the Father of the Western Monks
Answer Key to Comprehension Questions

Chapters 1 and 2—In Which Benedict Decides to Become a Hermit and Performs His First Miracle

1. Benedict left Rome as he felt the people there were only concerned about acquiring riches; he wanted to find a quiet place in the countryside where he could spend his days in prayer for those who would not pray for themselves.
2. Benedict felt that all the saints possessed an abundance of faith. He wanted to increase his own faith, and spend time honoring and loving God for all His goodness.
3. Benedict left Enfide as he felt his life there was too comfortable. He was also afraid of the reaction of Enfide's citizens to the miraculous mending of the sieve.

Chapters 3 and 4—Which Relate How Benedict Lived as a Hermit and How His Life as an Abbot at Vicovaro Was Brief

1. The virtues of faith and hope are the two virtues that belong to all great souls, including Benedict.
2. The monks of Vicovaro believed that the most important qualification for an abbot was that he be a man of prayer.
3. Benedict believed that obedience and humility were the virtues most important in leading a holy life.

Chapters 5 and 6—In Which Placid and Maurus Join the Monks at Subiaco, and Benedict Prays for the Three Monasteries atop the Mountain

1. Originally, twelve men joined Benedict in his colony at Subiaco.
2. Benedict's motto, in Latin, is *Ora et labora*, which means "pray and work."
3. According to Benedict, in order to have lasting happiness one must pay constant honor to God.

Chapters 7 and 8—In Which Three Miracles Occur, and Florentius Causes Benedict to Leave Subiaco

1. The three miracles of Chapter 7 include the finding of an abundant spring on top of the mountain where the three monasteries were located, the rescue of Placid from drowning, and the recovery of the scythe from the river.
2. Benedict decided to leave Subiaco in response to the unkindness of Florentius. This was in accordance with his motto: "Turn away from evil and do good. Seek after peace and pursue it" (page 59). [See Psalm 34 (33):15.]
3. Benedict left Subiaco as he felt it was the will of God. Maurus became abbot in his place.

Chapters 9 and 10—In Which Benedict Establishes the Monastery at Monte Cassino, and the Devil Causes Trouble

1. Benedict became a hermit again for several weeks in order to pray without distraction so God might enlighten his mind as to his next move. As a result, he decided to stay near Casinum and build a monastery on Monte Cassino, eighty miles south of Rome.
2. The devil, the father of jealousy and pride, was upset about Benedict's decision to build a monastery at Monte Cassino, as previously this place had been used as a place for devil worship; now it was being converted to a place of prayer to God. The devil used various means to thwart Benedict's work. He appeared to Benedict in hideous forms, shouted at and cursed Benedict, and caused numerous hardships including fires, increased the weight of the rocks the monks tried to remove, and caused accidents around the new monastery.
3. The miracle that occurred in Chapter 10 as a result of the intercession of Benedict was the raising of the boy Severus from the dead.

Chapters 11 and 12—In Which Benedict Writes His Rule and Teaches His Monks the Peace that Comes from Humility and Obedience

1. Benedict disapproved of Justinian's decision to wage war in Italy for several reasons: Benedict had no use for war as he saw it as a meaningless search for power and wealth with no true happiness attached. He also believed that the ordinary people would suffer greatly from the effects of war—young men would be killed, taxes would rise, and food would be scarce.

2. Benedict's Rule covered a variety of topics regarding the monastic life such as how to study, how to work, how to eat, how to sleep, and how to pray. It reinforced the monks' duty to praise God and to live by the motto of St. Benedict: *"Ora et labora"* (Pray and work).

Chapters 13 and 14—In Which Benedict's Monks Establish More Monasteries, and Benedict Teaches the Value of Obedience

1. Three gifts that Benedict received are mentioned in Chapter 13: A large estate at Terracina (page 88), a villa near the town of Aquinum (page 90), and the gift of eighteen farms in Sicily (page 90).

2. Benedict's advice to the monks who are leaving to start a new monastery in Terracina is simply to trust in God.

3. The three promises that Brother Michael had made when he came to Monte Cassino include the following: He promised to stay in the monastery for life, unless ordered by the abbot to go elsewhere; he promised to change his worldly ways and strive for perfection; and he promised to obey the abbot and his other superiors (page 100).

4. In Chapter 14, Brother Michael learned the importance of obedience as well as the importance of trusting in God's providence.

Chapters 15 and 16—In Which Benedict Shows the Power of Faith, Hope, and Charity

1. The following incidents are related as miracles attributed to Benedict in Chapter 15: The curing of a leper, finding thirteen shillings on top of the corn bin when needed for a man to pay his debt, sharing six loaves of bread while keeping five loaves to feed three hundred monks (and the deliverance the next day of two hundred bushels of meal to cover the shortage of grain), the strange unwinding of the peasant's wrist cords, he conversion of Zalla, and the raising of Paul's son from the dead.

2. Another name for the monastery on Monte Cassino was the School of the Lord's Service. (See the last paragraph of the Prologue of the Rule of St. Benedict.)

3. According the Brother Joseph, we conquer our weariness in the long struggle for perfection by considering ourselves a child and asking the Heavenly Father for strength and courage. The opportunity that awaits us when we feel most downhearted is the opportunity to practice great trust in God as our own strength and knowledge give way.

Chapters 17 and 18—In Which Benedict Proves Himself a Prophet to King Totila and Tells Maurus the Story of King Clovis

1. While at prayer Placid, along with thirty other monks as well as Placid's two brothers and sister—who were visiting Placid at the time—were tortured and killed by pirates in the early morning hours.

2. As he regarded the worldliness of man, Benedict begged God for His mercy and asked God to teach man these three things: the peace of His holy saints, love for one another, and forgiveness of our enemies.

3. Benedict prophesized to King Totila that he will reign over Italy for only nine more years and in the tenth year, he will die in a land across the sea.

4. In the letter Benedict gave to Maurus upon Maurus' departure from Monte Cassino, Benedict predicted the following: Maurus would govern the new monastery in France for thirty-eight years; he would then retire to a hermit's cell, and die shortly thereafter at the age of seventy-two. Benedict also foretold of his own death within the space of four years.

Chapters 19 and 20—In Which Benedict Reflects on the Path to Heaven and Sees into the Future

1. The vision that Benedict had on the night his friend Bishop Germanus of Capua died was a vision of his friend's soul entering paradise. He also saw the whole earth and all the people in it and was assured by God that men would continue to live under his Rule until the end of time.
2. The Benedictine monks, under the guidance of Benedict and the Rule, believed that manual labor is not only a great help to the body and spirit but also a way to attain humility—a ladder to heaven.
3. Benedict received a vision shortly before he died that caused him great sadness. In this vision, he saw the destruction of war upon the earth and mankind. He also saw the destruction of his monastery by the Lombards in 581—thirty-four years after his death.

Chapters 21 and 22—In Which Benedict Meets with Scholastica for the Last Time and Goes to His Eternal Reward

1. Benedict and his twin sister Scholastica wore similar habits—a dark tunic with scapular and belt. They also physically resembled each other. Both also had a great love of God.
2. As the time for her annual meeting with Benedict came near an end, Scholastica prayed for a storm of such magnitude that it would prevent Benedict and his monks from leaving. God granted her prayer immediately.
3. In Benedict's lifetime (480 to 547), much had happened in Italy. The invaders Odoacer and Theodoric had ruled much of that time. Then in 535, Emperor Justinian had invaded the country to revive the western Roman Empire and unite Italy with his holdings in the east. Currently King Totila was defeating Justinian's armies in a war that would last for twenty years (page 146). After a period of peace, the Lombards would invade Italy from the north—the same Lombards that would destroy Benedict's monastery at Monte Cassino in 581.
4. Benedict wished to be buried at Monte Cassino alongside his sister, Scholastica.

Answer Key to Book Summary Test

1. St. Benedict decided to leave his studies in Rome and become a hermit as he was unhappy in Rome; he felt there was too much emphasis on wealth and worldly things. He wanted the solitude of the countryside where he could devote his time to prayer.
2. St. Benedict left his hermit's life on two occasions. The first time he left as he was asked to become the abbot for the monks at Vicovaro. He then returned to his life as a hermit until the establishment of his colony at Subiaco where he taught the peasants to read and write, and to pray and work.
3. St. Benedict's motto was *"Ora et labora"*; the English translation from the Latin is "Pray and work." Much of his Rule is based upon this motto. In addition, he borrowed a motto from the book of Psalms, "Turn away from evil and do good. Seek after peace and pursue it" [Psalm 34 (33):15]. He also used a short motto: "Peace."
4. The prominent themes of St. Benedict's Rule are humility, obedience, and peace. He considered humility the ladder to heaven: "We must erect the ladder which appeared to Jacob in his dream, by means of which angels were shown to him ascending and descending. (cf Genesis 28:12) Without a doubt, we understand this ascending and descending to be nothing else but that we descend by pride and ascend by humility" (Rule of St. Benedict, Chapter 7).
5. Benedict lived shortly after the fall of the Rome empire. Various barbarian tribes were waging war and invading Italy. It was a time of violence, unrest, famine, and uncertainty. In this biography Mary Windeatt mentions several key figures of this time: Sts. Patrick, Augustine, Ambrose, Leo, Basil, and Gregory the Great; Emperors Justinian and Theodosius; and Kings Odoacer and Clovis.

Other RACE for Heaven Products

Catholic Study Guides for Mary Fabyan Windeatt's Saint Biography Series teach the Catholic faith to all members of your family. Written with your family's various learning levels in mind, these flexible study guides succeed as stand-alone unit studies or supplements to your regular curriculum. Thirty to sixty minutes per day will allow your family to experience:

- ☑ The spirituality and holy habits of the saints
- ☑ Lively family discussions on important faith topics
- ☑ Increased critical thinking and reading comprehension skills
- ☑ Quality read-aloud time with Catholic "living books"
- ☑ Enhanced knowledge of Catholic doctrine and the Bible
- ☑ History and geography incorporated into saintly literature
- ☑ Writing projects based on secular and Catholic historical events and characters

Purchase these guides individually or in the following grade-level packages. (Grade level is are determined solely on the length of each book in the series.)

Grades 3-4: *St. Thomas Aquinas, The Story of the "Dumb Ox"*; *St. Catherine of Siena, The Girl Who Saw Saints in the Sky*; *Patron Saint of First Communicants, The Story of Blessed Imelda Lambertini*; and *The Miraculous Medal, The Story of Our Lady's Appearances to St. Catherine Labouré*

Grade 5: *St. Rose, First Canonized Saint of the Americas*; *St. Martin de Porres, The Story of the Little Doctor of Lima, Peru*; *King David and His Songs, A Story of the Psalms*; and *Blessed Marie of New France, The Story of the First Missionary Sisters in Canada*

Grade 6: *St. Dominic, Preacher of the Rosary and Founder of the Dominicans*; *St. Benedict, The Story of the Father of the Western Monks*; *The Children of Fatima and Our Lady's Message to the World*; and *St. John Masias, Marvelous Dominican Gate-keeper of Lima, Peru*

Grade 7: *The Little Flower, The Story of St. Therese of the Child Jesus*; *St. Hyacinth, The Story of the Apostle of the North*; *The Curé of Ars, The Story of St. John Vianney, Patron Saint of Parish Priests*; and *St. Louis de Montfort, The Story of Our Lady's Slave*

Grade 8: *Pauline Jaricot, Foundress of the Living Rosary and the Society for the Propagation of Faith*; *St. Francis Solano, Wonder-Worker of the New World and Apostle of Argentina and Peru*; *St. Paul the Apostle, The Story of the Apostle to the Gentiles*; and *St. Margaret Mary, Apostle of the Sacred Heart*

The Windeatt Dictionary: Pre-Vatican II Terms and Catholic Words from Mary Fabyan Windeatt's Saint Biographies explains over 450 Catholic terms and expressions used in this popular saint biography series. Indispensable in expanding knowledge and practice of the Catholic faith, this book provides a ready access for the Catholic vocabulary words used in the RACE for Heaven Windeatt study guides. This dictionary also includes a Catholic book report resource that contains suggestions for forty-five Catholic book reports: fourteen writing projects, ten book report activities, and twenty-one topics for saint biographies.

Graced Encounters with Mary Fabyan Windeatt's Saints: 344 Ways to Imitate the Holy Habits of the Saints is a compilation of the "Growing in Holiness" sections of RACE for Heaven's Catholic study guides for the Windeatt saint biography series and presents 344 examples of saintly behavior, one for nearly every chapter in each of these twenty biographies. Enhance your encounter with the saints by practicing the models of devotion, service, penance, prayer, and virtue offered in this guide.

Bedtime Bible Stories for Catholic Children: Loving Jesus through His Word contains twenty discussions of Bible stories that were originally published in serial form in a Catholic children's magazine. Their author stated, "The tales are extremely simple and unadorned. They are real conversations of a real child and her mother." Due to popular demand, the series was later (1910) published as a book, *Bible Stories Told to "Toddles."* The engaging conversational style of this book lends itself well as a bedtime read-aloud that allows Jesus to come alive in the Gospels. The study aids include discussion questions to help foster spiritual conversation, Bible excerpts relevant to the presented story, "Growing in Holiness" suggestions for living the Gospel message in our daily lives, and short catechism lessons for both children and adults.

I Talk with God: The Art of Prayer and Meditation for Catholic Children strives to instill in young Catholics a love of prayer and a practical knowledge of the art of meditation. This prayer book contains prayers to pray out loud (vocal prayer) or in the silence of your heart. It shows how you can talk with God, and more importantly, how you can love God. As you progress through this book—from discovering what prayer is to reading and reciting simple prayers to understanding meditation and then to helps for deeper meditation—you will see that prayer and meditation often go together. Meditation is described by the big *Catechism of the Catholic Church* as nothing more than "prayerful reflection" or *holy thinking*. You can use books, devotions, pictures, holy cards, and images (such as the stained glass windows in church) to help you think about holy people, events, and ideas. Learn how to talk with God each day to increase your love for Him and follow more closely His holy will.

Communion with the Saints: A Family Preparation Program for First Communion and Beyond in the Spirit of St. Therese imitates St. Therese of the Child Jesus and her family who studied and prayed for sixty-nine days in anticipation of Therese's First Holy Communion. Modeling this preparation, the *Communion with the Saints* program will help any family find renewed fervor in the reception of the Eucharist. This resource includes a chapter-by-chapter study of the following four books:

- *The Little Flower, The Story of Saint Therese of the Child Jesus*—to provide the foundation of God's love for us and to encourage a desire for holiness

- *The Children of Fatima and Our Lady's Message to the World*—to show the sinfulness of our world and the need to avoid sin

- *The Patron Saint of First Communicants, The Story of Blessed Imelda Lambertini*—to inspire devotion to the Sacrament of Holy Communion

- *The King of the Golden City* by Mother Mary Loyola —to illustrate Jesus' Presence as a source of grace necessary to live a holy life

Each of the sixty-nine days of preparation includes read-aloud selections with enrichment activities, meditational readings, catechism lessons, and plenty of practical application to promote a growth in holiness and sanctity. Weekend suggestions include a list of over thirty-five family projects. The use of *My First Communion Journal* is encouraged with this program.

My First Communion Journal in Imitation of Saint Therese, The Little Flower provides a lasting keepsake of a child's First Holy Communion. This journal has been constructed in imitation of the copybook made for Therese Martin by her older sister Pauline to help Therese prepare for her First Holy Communion. Although this book is not an exact replica of the copybook used by Therese, it does contain many of the same prayers and aspirations she used, the same idea of flowers inspiring virtue, and the same method of recording prayers recited and sacrifices made. It is up to you to decorate and complete this journal, replicating Therese's heroic efforts by raising your mind and heart to Jesus and by humbling yourself with small sacrifices. Learn as well to imitate St. Therese's love and knowledge of Scripture as you meditate on—or even memorize—the biblical passages that are provided for reflection. This journal may be completed in conjunction with the *Communion with the Saints* program or used separately.

My First Communion Journal in Imitation of St. Paul, Putting on the Armor of God was also inspired by St. Therese's copybook and uses the same method of encouraging—and recording—daily prayers and mortifications. However, instead of using flowers to illustrate virtues, this resource uses the battle model St. Paul describes in Ephesians 6:10-17. First communicants are encouraged to arm themselves with virtues and spiritual weapons in order to fight as soldiers of Christ. The scriptural words of Jesus and St. Paul are reflected on frequently to encourage the imitation of the actions and love of Jesus and to inspire a love and knowledge of Holy Scripture. This journal too may be completed in conjunction with the *Communion with the Saints* program or used separately.

The King of the Golden City Study Edition is a new edition of a book that was originally published in 1921. This treasure of a book was written in response to a student's appeal for instructions along with "little stories" to help her prepare for Holy Communion. To fulfill this request, Mother Loyola of the Bar Convent in York, England, wrote a simple story that illustrates Jesus' desire to share an intimate relationship with each one of His children. This new edition contains some updated language but, quite deliberately, does not contain any pictures. Readers, as they progress through this story, will form a mental image of their King, one as unique and personal as their own relationship with Him. The study sections assist with the allegory, connect to the Bible as well as to the catechism, and explore the art of prayer in the spirit of the three Carmelite Doctors of the Church. Although written over ninety years ago for a young child, this book remains a timeless masterpiece of Catholic literature suitable for all ages. (Also available as a study guide only)

The Good Shepherd and His Little Lambs Study Edition is a simply told Catholic tale of four children who meet with their beloved aunt for "First Communion talks." More than a story, it is a First Communion primer that takes the tenets of the catechism and, through naturally-flowing conversations, relates them in the language of little ones to authentic Christian living. As Mrs. Bosch explains, "We might learn the catechism all the way through beautifully, and at the end find ourselves still very stiff and clumsy about loving our Lord. When He comes to us, we don't want to welcome Him into our souls only with answers out of the catechism, do we?" Enriched by appropriate Biblical passages, points of doctrine, and prayers, this story-primer is an enjoyable and effective read-aloud that will prepare the Good Shepherd's little lambs to worthily receive Him in the Holy Eucharist.

A Reconciliation Reader-Retreat: Read-Aloud Lessons, Stories, and Poems for Young Catholics Preparing for Confession provides a basic doctrinal explanation and review of the Sacrament of Reconciliation as well as a Gospel examination of conscience—a seven-day read-aloud formation retreat. To help the lessons come alive and to enable young Catholics to more readily apply these doctrines to their own daily lives, the lessons have been supplemented with pertinent short stories and poems. Each lesson contains reflection questions, a family prayer, and a "Gospel Examination of Conscience" that is formulated according to the dictates of the *Catechism of the Catholic Church*. This reader-retreat will not only enrich and deepen the sacramental experience for each member of your family but it will also provide several tools to help you recommit to leading a virtuous life and to grow together in holiness.

Devotion to St. Joseph: Read-Aloud Stories, Poems, and Prayers for Catholic Children encourages children to love Jesus as St. Joseph did. As Scripture does not record a single word this great saint spoke; we must take our lessons of his life from his actions. In this compilation of stories and poems about our Savior's foster-father from renowned Catholics, children of all ages are encouraged to imitate the virtues the life of St. Joseph reveal to us in his loving dedication to Jesus and Mary. The discussion questions as well as the reflections on the virtues of St. Joseph lead children to apply the lessons of this saint's life to their own while the prayer section promotes a lasting devotion to the great St. Joseph. As St. Teresa of Avila declared, "I wish I could persuade everyone to be devoted to this glorious saint!"

The Month of St. Joseph: Prayers and Practices for Each Day of March in Imitation of the Virtues of St. Joseph was originally published in 1874. This book contains daily meditations on the life and virtues of St. Joseph for adults and high-school students. In addition, each day presents a prayer to St. Joseph, several resolutions, a short ejaculatory prayer, a relevant Scripture verse, and a brief consideration for reflection. The practices for each day are intended to assist the reader in acquiring the habits of prayer and interior recollection so necessary to living in the presence of God. Perfect for Lenten reading, this journey through the life of St. Joseph reveals his love of God and neighbor, humility, quiet action, and spirit of sacrifice. While the Bible tells so little about St. Joseph's life, here we discover the abundant virtues of this silent saint—and are challenged to imitate them.

Alternative Book Reports for Catholic Students contains forty-five book report ideas to encourage critical thinking for ages seven to fourteen. These ideas are intended to provoke a reflection on those themes and topics that support and encourage Catholic living as well as some that may conflict with our Faith. Many report topics require an examination of our personal faith life and prompt us to take lessons from the saints to strengthen our own faith in God. The suggested activities vary from written exercises to creative art projects and include twenty-one topics specifically designed for saint biographies. Other activities can be used within a group or family.

Reading the Saints: Lists of Catholic Books for Children Plus Book Collecting Tips for the Home and School Library (formerly entitled *Saintly Resources*) is a valuable tool for Catholic home educators, classroom teachers, and collectors of Catholic juvenile books. This resource will help you discover living books from such popular out-of-print Catholic juvenile series as Catholic Treasury, Vision Books, and American Background Books as well as current series books for young Catholics. Use this book to find:

- Over 800 Catholic books listed by author, series, reading level, century, and geographical location
- More than 275 authors of saint biographies, historical fiction, and poetry written for Catholic juvenile readers
- Publishers of Catholic children's books, present and past
- Helpful advice for collecting and caring for used books
- Hundreds of age-appropriate, accessible living books to enrich your study of the Catholic Church's rich heritage of saints and notable Catholic historical figures
- Information on how to build and maintain your own library of Catholic juvenile books
- Inspiring quotations about book collecting, reading, and the love of books

The Outlaws of Ravenhurst Study Edition contains a classic story of the persecution of Scottish Catholics that was first written in 1923 and was revised and reprinted in 1950. This 2009 edition of Sr. M. Imelda Wallace's *Outlaws of Ravenhurst* contains the revised story of 1950 plus chapter-by-chapter aids to assist readers in assimilating the book's strong Catholic elements into their own lives. The study section focuses on critical thinking, integration of biblical teachings, and the study of the virtuous life to which Christ calls us as mature Catholics. With its emphasis on virtues (theological and moral plus the gifts and fruits of the Holy Spirit), the spiritual and corporal works of mercy, and the Beatitudes, *Outlaws of Ravenhurst Study Edition* is a fun and effective catechetical tool for Catholics preparing for the Sacrament of Confirmation. (Also available as a study guide only)

The Family that Overtook Christ Study Edition: The Story of the Family of St. Bernard of Clairvaux is an excellent read for young adults who are preparing to receive the Sacrament of Confirmation. In this exciting chronicle of the life of twelfth-century knights, we have an entire family of nine saints who lay before us their individual means of achieving intimate union with Christ. Learn with the Fontaines family how to supernaturalize the natural, develop a God-consciousness, and attain sanctity by being yourself. Perfect for high-school read-aloud (or adult study), this new study edition has over 250 footnotes for increased comprehension and provides discussion/meditation points to promote the art of spiritual conversation. The appendix lists formulas of Catholic doctrine that are essential for confirmands not only to know but also to incorporate into their own spiritual lives.

A Confirmation Reader-Retreat: Read-Aloud Lessons, Stories and Poems for Young Catholics utilizes chapters from two excellent out-of-print Catholic books for children (*I Belong to God, Great Truths in Simple Stories for Children and Lovers of Children* by Lillian Clark; and *Children's Retreats in Preparation for First Confession, First Holy Communion, and Confirmation* by Rev. P.A. Halpin). This book provides a basic doctrinal review of the Sacrament of Confirmation as well as prayer experiences—a nine-day read-aloud retreat/novena. The reprinted material has been supplemented with short stories and poems that provide insights in applying catechetical doctrines to the daily life of young Catholics. Each lesson concludes with "I Talk with God"—a section that encourages readers (of all ages) to deepen their relationship with each of the Three Persons of the Blessed Trinity. Reflection questions promote the habit of spiritual conversation within your family—to encourage family members to discuss holy topics—and to help you grow together in holiness. Additionally, a traditional novena to the Holy Spirit is included.

By Cross and Anchor Study Edition: The Story of Frederic Baraga on Lake Superior relates the exciting, and often miraculous, missionary adventures of the "Snowshoe Priest"—Venerable Frederic Baraga, the first bishop of Michigan's Upper Peninsula. Declared "Venerable" by Pope Benedict XVI on May 10, 2012, this priest came to the United States from Slovenia in 1830 to undertake his mission as a "simple servant of God." For almost forty years, Fr. Frederic Baraga traveled across over 80,000 square miles of wilderness by snowshoe in winter and canoe in summer. In imitation of Christ, Bishop Baraga become poor so that he might bring the riches of the Catholic Faith to the Chippewa and immigrant residents of the beautiful peninsula he served. Although not strictly a biography, this book is a story based on historical facts drawn from Bishop Baraga's own journal and letters—a fascinating, easy-to-read history of Michigan's northern peninsula. While this exciting adventure is intended for youth who are interested in knowing more about this quiet, courageous priest, readers of all ages will be inspired by his life of humility, simplicity, and selfless virtue. This new study edition contains over 130 footnotes, defining less familiar vocabulary words and—gleaned from Venerable Baraga's *Journal* and other primary sources—details regarding the region's people and places. Also included are discussion questions, applicable Scripture passages, pertinent quotations of Venerable Baraga from the text, and—most importantly—a section illustrating how to imitate the various virtues of Venerable Frederic Baraga. Additionally, the complete text of Bishop Baraga's 1853 "Pastoral Letter to the Faithful" has been included with numerous references added in order that we may read this in light of Scripture and the *Compendium of the Catechism of the Catholic Church*. Learn more about the life, ministry, and heroic virtues of Venerable Frederic Baraga, the "Snowshoe Priest."

To Order: Email info@RACEforHeaven.com or place an order at RACEforHeaven.com. Discover, MasterCard, VISA, PayPal, American Express, checks, and money orders are accepted.